RAP ON TRIAL

RAP ON TRIAL

RACE, LYRICS, AND GUILT IN AMERICA

ERIK NIELSON and
ANDREA L. DENNIS

with a foreword by
KILLER MIKE

THE
NEW
PRESS

NEW YORK
LONDON

Requests for permission to reproduce selections from this book should be made through our website: https://thenewpress.com/contact.

Published in the United States by The New Press, New York, 2019
Distributed by Two Rivers Distribution

ISBN 978-1-62097-340-0 (hc)
ISBN 978-1-62097-341-7 (ebook)
CIP data is available

The New Press publishes books that promote and enrich public discussion and understanding of the issues vital to our democracy and to a more equitable world. These books are made possible by the enthusiasm of our readers; the support of a committed group of donors, large and small; the collaboration of our many partners in the independent media and the not-for-profit sector; booksellers, who often hand-sell New Press books; librarians; and above all by our authors.

www.thenewpress.com

Book design and composition by Bookbright Media
This book was set in Minion Pro and Alternate Gothic

Printed in the United States of America

10 9 8 7 6 5 4 3 2 1

For my boyz

—Andrea L. Dennis

I dedicate this book to Sam, Mac, and Sandra

—Erik Nielson

CONTENTS

FOREWORD

It is difficult to overstate the influence of hip hop.

In the black community, it has been particularly important. For one, it has allowed many rappers—myself included—to become successful entrepreneurs, creating a new business class that has given us access to the American Dream. After the loss of a wide range of manufacturing jobs over the last several decades, hip hop has become a financial cornerstone for my community—one that extends far beyond the recording industry. It is, after all, a multibillion-dollar industry, one that provides opportunities for upward mobility within communities where such opportunities are far too rare.

At the same time, as an art form, it serves as a safe space where we can celebrate our blackness and each other—and be comfortable in our own skin while we do it. It has offered us a kind of therapy as well, a place to express even our rawest feelings.

And it has given us a way to say just things in unjust times.

That's why police and prosecutors' use of rap lyrics in criminal trials is of such grave concern. Left unchecked, it has the potential to silence a generation of artists who are exercising their First Amendment right to express themselves. These are voices we should be encouraging, yet our criminal justice system has consistently looked for ways to punish them.

As a kid, I saw the government try to criminalize the music of Luther Campbell and 2 Live Crew for "obscenity." I watched as the FBI and other law enforcement agencies targeted N.W.A for lyrics deemed too violent, too disrespectful of police. And I saw how police and politicians railed against Ice-T and Body Count for voicing the frustrations that many people in this country felt in the face of persistent police brutality. These are just a few examples of the concerted efforts by our government to silence hip hop artists, and as a young man the irony wasn't lost on me. As much of this was happening, I was in high school learning about the American Constitution and the Bill of Rights, which laid the groundwork for a republic that was—in theory anyway—radically different and vastly more free than others.

That was when I first began to understand that American law has a duality, regarding people differently not only based on race, but based on class and based on culture as well. On one hand, many artists from other musical genres—which can be just as dark and violent as rap can be—were being celebrated for their music, while rap artists were being vilified. And now we are seeing more and more examples where they are being prosecuted, sometimes for their lyrics alone.

I am sometimes asked whether this is all a big misunderstanding. Is it just that police don't understand hip hop, so they mistakenly view it as a threat? Are prosecutors treating violent rap lyrics as confessions of criminal behavior because they are simply ignorant about conventions of the genre?

The answer is no. Hip hop has become one of the most popular and influential genres of the last century. People understand it well enough. But prosecuting rap artists, who are predominantly young men of color, is politically expedient. Rap on trial is a continuation of what former vice president Joe Biden did in support of the 1994 crime bill warning America of "predators on the streets," young people "without any conscience developing" who needed to be removed from society. (The bill has been widely criticized as overly harsh and a major contributor to mass incarceration.) It has been expedient for politicians on both sides of the aisle to make the least of us the heel, the villain, the arch-nemesis of the established order.

Often, people don't care about what's just; they just care about order. They don't want it disrupted, and children from marginalized communities, particularly young men who call out injustice by saying "fuck government," are challenging the order that American society is comfortable with. Prosecutors know that locking up young men of color carries political capital, and they've figured out a way to use rap lyrics to do it.

Right now, aspiring rap artists need to know they are being targeted by the authorities, and they need to balance their right to free speech—and their desire to push the envelope of free speech—with the reality that police are watching. What scares me is that in some situations, such as the recent case involving Jamal Knox from Pittsburgh, a young rapper calls out police officers by name and directs threatening-sounding lyrics at them—and the courts use that as a reason to punish him. The court acts as though this kid just turned into a Navy Seal–trained hitman who is going to look up these officers' addresses, go to their houses, and kill their families, crime-movie style.

To those artists, I would say: you have to save yourself. Ask yourself how you can use your imagination to guard against this persecution while still pushing the line on speech. I'd take the *Law & Order* approach: take real stories and events, but change them up. If the police officer's real name is William Bradley, then change it to Bradford Williams.

Your imagination, which gives you the ability to express yourself freely, can also be used to protect yourself. So to younger artists, my advice is this: cloak your truth in some mystery, even as you keep pushing the line for absolute freedom of speech. In this environment, that's the best thing you can do.

But we also need to change the environment that makes such measures necessary. That's what *Rap on Trial* is trying to do, first and foremost by giving historical context to the injustices that are happening right now. It is also giving name and voice to many of the people who are suffering as a result of those injustices. And I appreciate that. Because black men are too often our martyrs and messiahs, uncredited. We are often lost in the pages of history, and this book is taking a small but meaningful step toward changing that.

Right now young men who sing and rap and rhyme are suffering for their ability to say what they want to. We all benefit from the artists who push the boundaries of speech, and so as a country we should see a collective interest in protecting them. This is especially true for artists who criticize the state, because once the state—which is supposed to be a representation of the people—is above reproach, we are entering Orwellian waters.

That scares the shit out of me.

For black Americans, the stakes are particularly high. If you want to know how society is going to treat people under the law, look first at how they treat the most marginalized, the people that are in the minority. African Americans, the descendants of slaves, are the petri dish for what the law is going to do. If we don't hold the line on our freedom of speech and the right to express ourselves as artists, we will be the first people dragged off to jail.

As this book documents, it's already starting to happen, and that's why I am in this fight.

Michael Render (aka Killer Mike)

RAP ON TRIAL

INTRODUCTION

McKinley Phipps was something of a prodigy. Born into a family of artists and raised in New Orleans's Third Ward, Phipps always had a gift for words. As a boy, he began writing poetry, which he sometimes recited at local coffee shops, but by the late 1980s, as rap music was becoming a national sensation, he saw the chance to turn his love for words into a career.

At age eleven, he released his first video, rapping as "Lil Mac." Then in 1990, at the age of thirteen, he released his first album, *The Lyrical Midget*. Featuring production from fellow New Orleans artist Mannie Fresh, who would go on to become one of hip hop's most celebrated producers, it was one of the earliest commercial hip hop efforts to emerge from New Orleans.

One of the songs from the album, "I Need Wheels," captures the frustration that many children experience when they long for independence they can't have. Straddling the line between his aspirations and his reality, Lil Mac raps about needing a car of his own, even though he's several years too young to drive. And he claims to have women all across the city, even as he's begging his father to buy him a car so he can visit them: "So Daddy buy me a car / I got too many girlfriends that live too far / And then every weekend I'm stuck at home / With this fine girl teasing me on the telephone."

On the surface, it's a song about a kid who wants a car so he can meet girls. It's a song that teens from all walks of life can relate to. But it also speaks to the sense of being trapped that Phipps, and many kids in the poorer neighborhoods of New Orleans, felt on a daily basis.[1] By

1990, the city was experiencing record levels of violent crime and had one of the highest black poverty rates among large cities in America. As such, it offered limited opportunities for upward mobility to young black men, so Lil Mac's fear that without a car he might be "stuck at home" would have resonated in a community where being "stuck" often meant being poor, in prison, or worse.

Ironically, Phipps had already found the vehicle he needed to escape: rap music. His debut record not only rode the rising tide of rap music across the country but also foreshadowed the rise of New Orleans as a hip hop mecca, thanks in large part to the success of No Limit Records, founded by rapper Master P. At its peak in the 1990s, No Limit was producing albums at a dizzying pace and was expanding its roster to include the likes of Mystikal and Snoop Dogg. In 1998 alone, No Limit released twenty-three albums and sold nearly 15 million copies.[2]

One of those albums, *Shell Shocked*, belonged to Phipps, now rapping as Mac. He had declined offers from bigger labels, such as New York's Def Jam Recordings, to join No Limit, and he was quickly recognized as one of the most talented lyricists on the label. While he never led a life of crime himself, Mac was skilled at producing the gritty, often violent lyrics that helped No Limit sell records. As Mac himself noted in a 2016 interview, "We're in this to make this money, and we're feeding a market that demands this type of content. At the end of the day, I wasn't walking around shooting people in real life, and I wasn't walking around selling drugs to people in real life. . . . I made the kind of music I made because to me at that time it appeared to be the most lucrative route."[3]

After hearing the lyrics in *Shell Shocked*, delivered by a rapper who sometimes called himself "The Camouflage Assassin," listeners probably would've been surprised to learn that Mac had no criminal record whatsoever and that he was, in fact, a mild-mannered young man who liked to read poetry and still called his father "Daddy." Likewise, most people would've been surprised to learn that No Limit Records, with its stable of flashy artists who were rapping about guns and drugs, was actually a highly disciplined, tightly run business. Master P had an incredible knack for anticipating the demands of his audience, and he was able to meet those demands quickly, sometimes recording and releasing an album in just a few weeks.[4] To make the No Limit system work, he demanded discipline from his artists as well, forcing them to stay as focused on the end game as he was.

That end game, of course, was money, and No Limit was making a lot of it. By 1999, Master P made *Fortune* magazine's "40 Richest Under 40" list, with an estimated net worth of $361 million.[5] He was just twenty-nine years old. While much of the country didn't know who he was or that his No Limit enterprise had grown to include a wide range of other businesses, he and the No Limit family were certainly well known in New Orleans. They flaunted their money and celebrated their success openly. When Master P bought a mansion in Baton Rouge's exclusive Country Club of Louisiana, next to former Louisiana governor Edwin Edwards, many saw the improbable and inspiring rise of a black kid from the projects of New Orleans who had made it to the highest levels of power.

But many others saw something different. They saw black men getting rich off a form of entertainment they considered an affront to "traditional" American values. And they saw a group of black men who weren't afraid to call attention to police harassment, abuse, and corruption. One of Master P's earliest songs, "Crooked Ass Law," set the tone for subsequent songs from the No Limit label, which were sometimes openly critical of and defiant toward the police. In "Runnin' from the Police," a song by C-Murder (Master P's brother) and No Limit labelmate Mystikal, C-Murder raps, "Every time I see the boys in blue / I wanna run and get the gun and start bustin' for fun."

Perhaps unsurprisingly, No Limit artists often found themselves the targets of police surveillance and harassment. Just driving a short distance could be provocation for a police stop. In a recent interview, Baton Rouge rapper Lil Boosie (who now raps as Boosie Badazz), also known for being critical of the police in his songs, spoke to the way he and others were routinely singled out by police. One time, for example, police pulled Boosie over, and before letting him go, they threw thousands of dollars of his cash across a freeway. Another time they took a knife to the upholstery in his car, just to make a point.[6]

In that kind of environment, it makes sense that Master P and his artists would adopt military imagery in their aesthetic, most obvious in their penchant for camouflage clothing. Perhaps they saw themselves as soldiers in a culture war, with camouflage signaling their recognition that visibility can create vulnerability.

No artist came to realize that more than Mac.

On the night of February 20, 2000, he was performing during an open mic night at Club Mercedes in Slidell, Louisiana, a small venue about thirty miles outside of New Orleans. A fight broke out in the tightly packed crowd, and a young fan, Barron Victor Jr., was shot and killed in the melee. When he heard the gunshots, Mac initially made his way to the back door before returning inside the club to make sure his parents, who were there collecting money for the performance, were safe. He drew his own (legally registered) gun for protection, meaning witnesses saw him with a gun in his hand, a fact that authorities seized on. They immediately identified Mac as the primary suspect and arrested him later that evening.

The ensuing process was a nightmare.[7] Numerous witnesses at the scene had described a shooter who looked nothing like Mac. The gun Mac was carrying hadn't been fired, and police never recovered the weapon that had been. No other forensic evidence tied Mac to the crime. *Another man even went to police and confessed to the shoot-*

ing. Nevertheless, authorities charged Mac—who had no criminal record—with first-degree murder. At trial they produced a number of their own eyewitnesses who, nearly fifteen years later, recanted their testimony completely, revealing that prosecutors threatened to put them in jail if they didn't finger Mac as the shooter. One of them, a pregnant woman named Yulon James, was told she could identify Mac as the killer or have her baby in prison.[8]

The trial itself, taking place just weeks after the September 11, 2001, attacks, revealed just how damaging Mac's rap career was to his case. The prosecutor took great pains to depict him as the brutal character in his songs. Taking full advantage of people's fear and anxiety after 9/11, he intentionally repeated Mac's moniker—the Camouflage Assassin, a name inspired by Mac's love of kung fu movies—throughout the trial. And he quoted liberally from Mac's 1998 album. "This defendant who did this is the same defendant whose message is, 'Murder murder, kill, kill, you fuck with me you get a bullet in your brain,'" the prosecutor said during his closing argument. "You don't have to be a genius to figure out that one plus one equals two."[9]

Jurors didn't know the prosecutor had selectively grabbed quotes from different songs, juxtaposing lyrics in a way Phipps never intended. Phipps was rapping about his Vietnam veteran father in the song "Shell Shocked" with the line "Big Mac, that's my daddy, rotten dirty straight up soldier . . . You fuck with me, he'll give you a bullet in your brain." The lyrics do not even contain the line "you fuck with me you get a bullet in your brain," as the prosecutor claimed. And the line "Murder, murder, kill, kill" is from a different song altogether.

Louisiana is a special place. Aside from consistently vying for the title of America's (and therefore the world's) incarceration capital, until very recently it was one of two states where jury verdicts didn't have to be unanimous to convict (the other is Oregon).[10] In a throwback to Jim Crow, Louisiana permitted guilty verdicts even if up to two (out of twelve) jurors found a defendant not guilty.[11] In November 2018, Louisiana voters finally passed a constitutional amendment requiring unanimous verdicts in all felony trials.

That change would have led to a very different outcome for Mac. That's because even after the all-white jury was exposed to coerced witnesses and a barrage of mangled rap lyrics, two jurors held out. Today that would've been enough to avoid a guilty verdict, but in 2001 it wasn't. Mac was convicted of manslaughter, a lesser charge, and was sentenced to thirty years in prison, a term he is still serving despite mountains of evidence that he was wrongly convicted. He refuses to accept parole because that would require him to admit his guilt first.

Years after the verdict, the jury foreman revealed in an interview that the lyrics presented to the jury certainly helped inform their decision. "The music—the lyrics—they played all that shit [in court]," he said. "I don't listen to that shit, but the music might have been the problem. The rap got his mind all messed up. He was living a life that he thought he was a gangsta. He was making it big time with the gold chains and all that shit that went with it. To shoot somebody in a public place on the dance floor, you gotta think you're a bad son of a bitch."[12]

One might forgive Mac if he eventually succumbed to bitterness after serving nearly twenty years in prison for a crime he almost certainly didn't commit. But that's not Mac. Still gentle and mild-mannered, he has been a model inmate and a man with seemingly endless patience in a system that has been content to throw men like him away.

In a telling postscript, in the years following Mac's incarceration, both C-Murder (Master P's brother) and Lil Boosie were also charged with murder. In both cases, authorities used, or attempted to use, their lyrics and rap images against them.

Boosie was lucky; he was acquitted. C-Murder was not. He is serving a life sentence, even as the eyewitnesses against him, as in Mac's case, have recanted their testimony, claiming that police, who were openly hostile to rap music, coerced them all along.[13] Former No Limit label-mates, C-Murder and Mac are now being housed in the same Louisiana prison, a reminder that in America's police culture, rapping can be a very dangerous business.

Stories like these are playing out all across the country: with alarming regularity, young men are finding themselves in handcuffs, in courtrooms, and often in prison because of their rap lyrics. Rather than acknowledging that these lyrics are the result of creative license, the criminal justice system has effectively denied rap music the status of art, allowing police and prosecutors to present it to juries as autobiography rhymed over a beat—often with devastating consequences.

No other fictionalized form, musical or otherwise, is treated this way in court. That's why we call this book *Rap on Trial*. It's not art on trial. It's not music on trial. It's only rap.

From its origins in the streets of the Bronx, New York, in the late 1970s, rap music has emerged into today's mainstream. Once an outsider musical art form predicted to have a short lifespan, rap music is now the most listened-to genre in the United States. It has become part of a multibillion-dollar industry, one used to market products as common and diverse as sneakers, soda, deodorant, internet service, clothing, food and alcohol, headphones, sports drinks, automobiles, water, and cellphones.[14]

With commercial success has come critical acclaim as well. Rap lyrics are included in numerous literary anthologies, taught at major universities, and acknowledged by even the most traditional institutions for their imagination and sophistication. In 2018, for example, Kendrick Lamar, one of rap's most commercially successful artists, was awarded the Pulitzer Prize in Music for his album *DAMN.*, which the Pulitzer committee described as "a virtuosic song collection unified by its vernacular authenticity and rhythmic dynamism that offers affecting vignettes capturing the complexity of modern African-American life."[15]

Modern rap music is a rich, complex art form. Research tells us that listening to and creating rap music can be a healthy aspect of adolescence and young adulthood. At the most basic level, it can simply serve as a creative and entertaining outlet. But it also can facilitate identity development, support emotional intelligence, and provide a safe space for experimentation. For these reasons and others, hip hop–based education has become increasingly influential in secondary and postsecondary contexts.[16] In many other contexts—social, educational, and clinical—hip hop is a powerful therapeutic tool.[17] And listening to hip hop has been shown to increase youth involvement in social and political activism.[18]

For many youth, beyond just personal development, writing rap music is a way to make a living and advance their social and economic standing. Becoming a rapper is a legitimate professional goal, particularly for individuals who are otherwise shut out of the economic mobility game. Even those who don't become the next Jay-Z or Kendrick Lamar—two of rap's most successful artists—have a wide range of career opportunities open to them. Hip hop is, after all, big business.

Despite all these prosocial aspects, kids who produce or listen to rap are often viewed as dangerous or antisocial. Particularly in public spaces, such misperceptions can leave kids vulnerable.

Consider Jordan Davis. In November 2012, seventeen-year-old Davis, who was black, was shot and killed by Michael Dunn, a white man. Dunn was infuriated by Davis and his three friends, who were playing rap music loudly through the speakers of their car stereo at a Florida gas station. Dunn had pulled his vehicle into the station, adjacent to the boys' vehicle. Dunn allegedly said to his girlfriend, who was in the car, "I hate that thug music," or referred to the music as "rap crap."[19] Dunn asked that the music be turned down, and an argument began when the boys refused. Dunn subsequently opened fire on the vehicle from the outside, killing Davis, who was seated in the rear of the vehicle. No gun or weapon was found in the car. Dunn claimed he acted in self-defense because Davis was threatening him with a gun or stick and he feared for his life. After two trials, Dunn was convicted of murder.

Or consider Michael Brown, whose interest in rap caused him to be demonized in the news media. In the early morning hours of August 9, 2014, eighteen-year-old Brown was shot and killed by white police officer Darren Wilson. Shortly after, on the day of Brown's funeral, a *New York Times* article about Brown painted a picture of him as a troubled youth and referred to him as "no angel."[20] The article chronicled Brown's alleged criminal history, drug and alcohol use, and even his residence in "a community that had rough patches." To complete the picture of Brown's problems, the article described his interest in rap music. Brown reportedly "had taken to rapping in recent months, producing lyrics that were by turns contemplative and vulgar." The article then quoted one of Brown's lyrics: "My favorite part is when the bodies hit the ground." Of course, there were softer lyrics in which Brown complained of deadbeat dads and doted on his stepmother. But those didn't reinforce the narrative of Brown as a monster. After the article was published, criticism came swiftly, and the author subsequently expressed regret over his choice of words. While this particular article may have struck a nerve, this was nothing new in the media or, it turns out, the courtroom.

Many people know the stories of Jordan Davis and Michael Brown.[21] But there are far more stories that people don't know, particularly those happening with little fanfare inside criminal courtrooms across

America. In these spaces, judges and prosecutors routinely reject rap music as a worthwhile enterprise. They read lyrics without context, ignoring the artistic conventions and the prospect of personal gain that should inform their interpretations. Moreover, they regularly overlook rap as a normal, healthy, positive aspect of life: defendants can simply enjoy or create the music without malicious motives, for fun, as a way to work through difficult emotions or experiences, or to improve their personal or financial status. Instead, these judges and prosecutors seem driven by a desire to convict and incarcerate.

Rap on trial is a dangerous trend we should pay attention to for several reasons. Most importantly, it contributes to society's ongoing willingness to target, incarcerate, and dehumanize already vulnerable black and Latino men. It has disrupted the lives of countless young men, inserting them into the criminal justice system in a way that forever alters their future. What's more, the tactic is spawning a modern resurgence of the use of racial epithets and racial images in the trial process—a practice which has long been shunned—in the process undermining the legitimacy and fairness of the criminal justice system. Finally, rap on trial mutes a current generation of rappers who find themselves behind bars, out of public view, and may intimidate current and future generations of rappers who fear criminal justice consequences as a result of their lyrics.

In the end, we aren't trying to convince you to like rap music. We aren't claiming that everyone in the pages to follow is innocent of every crime they're accused of. Our goal is more basic than that. It's to demonstrate that in courtrooms across the nation, people are being denied a fair trial in a particularly insidious way.

Andrea first encountered this issue in the early 2000s when she worked as an assistant federal public defender, representing indigent clients charged with federal crimes. Another attorney in the office had a client who was an aspiring rapper. The client had been charged with homicide, and songs he had recorded were among the pieces of evidence against him. That case was resolved with the songs playing little role in the outcome, but it signaled something alarming to Andrea. Fast-forward to 2006, when she was a new law professor at the University of Kentucky in Lexington. A colleague mentioned that the Taquan Neblett capital trial was ongoing in a local courthouse. Neblett was charged with murdering a music store clerk during a 2004 robbery, and he was facing the death penalty.

The prosecutor sought to rely on lyrics purportedly written by Neblett on the day of his arrest, weeks after the killing:

So any nigga in the path to the flow of my cash
Will find that breathing is a privilege when taking your last

At trial, the prosecutor argued that the graphic and violent nature of the lyrics was a "reflection" of Neblett's "soul" and should be admitted to prove Neblett's guilt. The court rejected the argument and refused to admit the lyrics. After the jury convicted Neblett, however, the court admitted the lyrics during the capital sentencing phase. There the prosecutor argued to the jury, "Just because you write lyrics doesn't mean they have true meaning. Johnny Cash was never really in Folsom Prison and didn't shoot his old lady down. But defendant is living his lyrics." The jury recommended a death sentence. Because of juror misconduct during the trial, however, the court sentenced Neblett to life without the possibility of parole for twenty-five years.[22]

After recalling the earlier case from her career and following the Neblett case, Andrea determined that there was something worth examining more deeply. Her research resulted in a 2007 academic law review article that defined the scope of the practice to date, analyzed the lawfulness of the practice in light of evidence rules and the small body of existing social science, and proposed solutions, including the use of defense expert testimony. Since that time, she has continued to follow the issue and collaborate with Erik.

For more than a decade, Erik's research has focused on the complex relationship between black art and the law in the United States. In 2011, as part of that research, he began coming across more and more cases in which rap music was being used as evidence in criminal cases. A handful involved artists who were fairly well known (at least to hip hop fans)—Louisiana rapper Lil Boosie (now Boosie Badazz), Philadelphia rapper Beanie Sigel, and California rapper X-Raided, to name a few. But then scores of cases involving amateur artists across the country began to turn up.

To get a better sense of what was happening, Erik began reaching out to the defense attorneys who represented these rappers. When they learned about his Ph.D. in English and that much of his teaching and scholarship centered on hip hop, they began to ask if he'd be willing to help, either by consulting or by serving as an expert witness. Eager to see the criminal process up close and to understand exactly how rap lyrics were being permitted as evidence, he agreed. Since then, he's worked on roughly fifty cases across the country, serving as an expert in more than a dozen of them.

Once it became clear that rap on trial was pervasive, he wanted to consider it systemically. That's how he found Andrea, who was one of the first scholars to write about it. For the last several years, they've been working together to raise awareness about a problem they both agree has frightening implications for our criminal justice system.

Over the last ten years, we have been seeking out and documenting cases of rap on trial. To date we have identified approximately five hundred from across the nation and in both state and federal courts. Finding these cases hasn't been easy. We found many of them through searches of legal case databases and media reporting. We learned of many others from attorneys who had pending cases and were seeking expert assistance. And, sad to say, some we learned of from attorneys who discovered our work only *after* they had a rap on trial case. We continue to look for cases, confident that there are far more closed cases than we have identified out there and, unfortunately, more cases coming in the future. We regularly hear about cases in which prosecutors use a single rap video to indict various people who happened to appear in it, even if they were just standing or dancing in the background. If those cases ended in plea bargains, as many do, there are likely no online records to search because the case didn't go to trial. And if we're hearing stories like this routinely, we know that even with the hundreds of cases we have identified, there are far more we haven't. In the meantime, our current collection of rap on trial cases forms the basis for this book.

Those cases reveal that there are a few basic scenarios in which prosecutors use rap lyrics as criminal evidence. These aren't rigid categories, and there's sometimes overlap between them, but they help conceptualize the practice.

The diary. One of the most common scenarios occurs when prosecutors treat a defendant's lyrics as rhymed confessions. Take, for example, the 2012 trial of Alex Medina, a fourteen-year-old boy charged as an adult with first-degree murder in Ventura, California. Medina was an aspiring rapper, and in the course of his arrest, police seized his notebooks full of lyrics, as well as recordings he had made. At trial, the prosecutor claimed that the most violent lyrics in the songs were "autobiographical journals" containing numerous admissions of guilt.[23] It didn't matter that the lyrics were written in verse and were clearly inspired by well-known rappers or weren't even written by Medina (he had copied down lyrics to some of his favorite songs, which were then characterized erroneously as his own). They were presented to the jury as confessions of previous acts. In the end, he was convicted and sentenced to twenty-five years to life, the maximum possible. During sentencing, the judge called Medina a "psychopath."

Motive and intent. If the lyrics were written or performed by the defendant *before* the alleged crime, prosecutors have to change their argument somewhat. The lyrics obviously cannot be an after-the-fact confession, so prosecutors instead argue that the lyrics are evidence of the defendant's identity, motive, intent, or knowledge with respect to the crime.

Take, for instance, a seminal case dating back to 1991, one of the earliest cases we've found involving rap lyrics as evidence, *United States v. Foster*. The defendant, Derek Foster, was caught by police at Chicago's Union Station transporting large quantities of drugs in suitcases. Foster denied that he knew the drugs were in the suitcases, but he did admit that a notebook he was carrying belonged to him. The notebook had rap lyrics he had written, which included the line "Key for Key, Pound for pound I'm the biggest Dope Dealer and I serve all over town." These were later introduced as evidence of Foster's knowledge of drug terminology and the drug business; he was ultimately convicted of possession with intent to distribute.

On appeal, Foster's attorneys argued that the lyrics were pure fiction, consistent with popular rap at the time, and therefore never should have been admitted as evidence. But the Seventh Circuit U.S. Court of Appeals said they were admissible as evidence, noting that "in writing about this 'fictional' character, Foster exhibited knowledge of an activity that is far from fictional. He exhibited some knowledge of narcotics trafficking, and in particular drug code words." The court didn't consider the possibility that Foster learned these terms from popular culture, the way many of us do.

Foster is just one example of how rap lyrics are used as evidence of a defendant's mind-set with respect to a crime. Other examples include cases in which songs authored by a defendant, or even another person, are used to show a defendant's gang associations, knowledge of firearms, knowledge of criminal activity, or involvement in other illegal activities.

Threats. There's one final scenario in which rap lyrics are introduced as evidence: when they are considered threats. Unlike the previous scenarios, in which the lyrics are used to establish the defendant's role in some underlying crime, in threats cases, the lyrics themselves are the crime. Here, police and prosecutors argue that rap lyrics should be understood as literal threats directed at another person or group of people. "True threats" are not protected under the First Amendment, and so they can be legitimately criminalized. Threats cases are a relatively small subset of what we've found, but they have been growing over the last decade, thanks in large part to antiterrorism laws passed after 9/11, but also to the growth of social media.

In fact, the highest-profile case involving rap as evidence, *Elonis v. U.S.*, was a threats case that played out over social media and was ultimately heard by the U.S. Supreme Court. *Elonis* dates to 2010, when twenty-seven-year-old Anthony Elonis began posting violent messages to Facebook, often in rap lyric form, that were directed at his estranged wife and, once the FBI got involved, a female agent who was investigating his actions.[24] Elonis insisted that he was merely writing lyrics that were consistent with the conventions of rap music; at one point he singled out rapper and fifteen-time Grammy winner Eminem—who is well known for hurling lyrical threats at his ex-wife—as one of his influences.[25] He also included caveats in the posts themselves that he was using the lyrics in an artistic sense.

But prosecutors argued that the lyrics were literal threats, not art, and ultimately the jury agreed. Elonis was found guilty and sentenced to forty-four months in prison.[26] The U.S. Supreme Court later overturned the verdict based on the law governing the definition of a true threat. The justices didn't make any decisions on the broader First Amendment questions about rap, art, and freedom of speech.

Whether charged as a threat or used as evidence of a crime, the common denominator is the claim by police and prosecutors that rap lyrics are accurate reflections of a defendant's thoughts, intentions, or actions. Rarely do they acknowledge—as they do with films, novels, and other musical genres—that there's a distinction between the author and the narrator telling the story. Consider how that would play out if this happened with other forms of entertainment. Crime novelists, radical poets, and screenwriters of horror films would all be in serious trouble if we could be convinced that their art was a reflection of their real lives.

The rules of evidence that govern criminal cases generally protect these other artists. But those rules are not applied in the same way to rap music unless the defendant is famous. The vast majority of defendants confronted with their rap lyrics are amateurs, who at best have achieved local or regional success. They are not nationally or internationally known and do not perform in major concert venues, if they even perform onstage. But the fame level of the defendant and whether the defendant performs in highly public settings influence how police, prosecutors, and courts evaluate lyrics and assess their admissibility in court. If the defendant is famous or performs the lyrics in concert settings, then the lyrics are readily deemed fictional, fantastical, and for pure entertainment. If the defendant is not famous, then the lyrics are deemed true depictions of life. In other words, defendants who are famous rappers are extended artistic respect and creative license, while amateurs are presumed to be rapping about their real lives, as if they have little artistic ability or aim. But there is no rational reason to distinguish between defendants based merely on whether they are aspiring or famous. And certainly fame shouldn't determine whether someone is treated fairly by the criminal justice system. But it does.

For amateur rappers, this lack of protection leaves them exposed, and prosecutors take full advantage, using it as an opportunity to convince judge and jury alike that the defendant is actually living the lifestyle depicted in the lyrics. If the song in question has vivid depictions of violence and other illicit activity, the jury will see a criminal underneath.

That's not just our take. A revealing excerpt from a training manual written by a California prosecutor includes this description of a generic defendant: "Invariably, by the time the jury sees the defendant at trial, his hair has grown out to a normal length, his clothes are nicely tailored, and he will have taken on the aura of an altar boy. But the *real* defendant is a criminal wearing a do-rag and throwing a gang sign."[27] Notice the assumption that the "real defendant," one who's supposedly presumed innocent at this stage, is already proclaimed a criminal. And the "do-rag" reference gives us a pretty good idea of what he might look like, too.

To uncover the real criminal, the manual advises that "through photographs, letters, notes, and *even music lyrics*, prosecutors can invade and exploit the defendant's true personality."[28]

We don't believe prosecutors should be able to use rap music this way. Some evidence is useful in determining guilt or innocence—that is, it has *probative value*. Other evidence has the potential to cause a jury to act in an emotional or irrational way regardless of the evidence—it could have an unfairly *prejudicial impact*. To ensure a fair trial for the defendant, prosecutors shouldn't be allowed to introduce evidence if its prejudicial impact substantially and unfairly outweighs its probative value. Rap music is an art form, told in rhymed verse, that privileges figurative language and resides in a long tradition of hyperbolic rhetoric. It has little, if any, probative value. At the same time, research has shown over and over that rap lyrics are likely to be highly prejudicial and inflammatory, particularly the violent, hyperaggressive lyrics that are generally at issue in cases like these. Some people simply don't like rap music, and for many, the genre invokes racist stereotypes about the inherent criminality of young black and Latino men.

Social science confirms the bias against rap in comparison to country music, which has many of the same themes. In a 1999 study, for example, participants were divided into two groups and then given song lyrics that contained depictions of violence (they were from a folk song). Both groups were given the exact same lyrics, but one group was told that they came from a country song, while the other group was told they came from a rap song. The group that believed the lyrics were from a rap song rated them as more dangerous and in need of regulation than the group that was told the lyrics were from a country song. The researcher posited that the differences were rooted in racial stereotypes; rap music primes negative stereotypes about urban blacks, while country music, in which white artists predominate, does not. In 2016, this study was replicated by researchers from the University of California–Irvine, who found the same bias against rap.

Age may also play a significant role in the practice of rap on trial. In particular, data confirms that most criminal defendants are young adult males, but jurors, in contrast, tend to be quite a bit older. This age disparity potentially translates into a difference in appreciation for and understanding of rap music, both generally and in the trial context. After all, rap has become the most popular musical genre overall but falls out of the top spot among older age groups, and data suggests that older people are more likely to have negative views of rap music than of other musical genres.[29]

Not surprisingly, our research has found that the defendant in these cases is almost always a young man of color. Based on the data we have collected, we estimate that in 95 percent of these cases the defendant is either black or Latino. While we do, on occasion, encounter cases with white defendants, these are the exception, not the rule. What's more, it's worth noting that in the handful of cases involving white defendants, the outcome is often more favorable for the defense. In *Elonis*, the threats case, the Supreme Court ultimately ruled in Elonis's favor. Elonis is white.

In another case, an eighteen-year-old from Boston named Cameron D'Ambrosio was charged with making threats with his lyrics after the Boston Marathon bombing. If convicted, he faced up to twenty years in prison, but prosecutors couldn't even convince a grand jury to indict him. He walked free. He is also white.[30]

For black and Latino defendants, however, the outcomes are often devastating. In the majority of cases we've identified, rap lyrics are being used to prosecute serious crimes including murder, armed robbery, and narcotics trafficking. In some of the cases, the evidence—putting aside the lyrics—is incredibly weak. And when defendants are found guilty, as they usually are, the consequences are severe. Many face terms that are decades long. Others are sentenced to life in prison without the possibility of parole. And we've found nearly thirty cases where rap lyrics were introduced to help prosecutors secure death sentences.

When prosecutors are allowed to introduce rap music as evidence, they often gain a stranglehold on the case. That's because rap lyrics allow them to create a narrative about the defendant that is incredibly difficult to undo. Even with a weak case, they can usually win a conviction.

Take the case of Vonte Skinner, a New Jersey drug dealer and aspiring rapper. In 2008, he was tried for the attempted murder of fellow drug dealer Lamont Peterson.[31] When Skinner was arrested, police found pages of his violent rap lyrics in the backseat of his girlfriend's car. With lines like "In the hood, I am a threat / It's written on my arm and signed in blood on my Tech / I'm in love with you, death," prosecutors were eager to introduce the lyrics at trial to establish Skinner's "violent state of mind." That's because their case was weak; the only other real evidence they had was testimony from witnesses who changed their stories repeatedly.

During the trial, over repeated objections from the defense, the prosecutor was allowed to read to the jury thirteen pages of Skinner's lyrics, even though all were composed before the shooting—in many cases *years* before—and none of them mentioned the victim or contained details about the crime. The tactic worked. The jury found Skinner guilty of attempted murder, and he was later sentenced to thirty years in prison.

But in 2012, Skinner's conviction was overturned by an appellate court, which ruled that the lyrics never should have been admitted as evidence in the first place. The majority wrote, "We have a significant doubt about whether the jurors would have found defendant guilty if they had not been required to listen to the extended reading of these disturbing and highly prejudicial lyrics." In August 2014, the Supreme Court of New Jersey unanimously upheld the appellate court's decision.

That's a rare victory. In the vast majority of cases, rap lyrics are admitted, and appeals are unsuccessful. The New Jersey ACLU, for instance, found that in cases where various courts considered the admissibility of rap lyrics as evidence, they were allowed nearly 80 percent of the time.[32] Their data analysis came from a very small sampling of cases, however. Our research, which has the benefit of a much larger sample of cases, leads us to the conclusion that the number is significantly higher. Appeals of criminal convictions are unsuccessful generally, and appealing the use of rap music as evidence virtually never works.

Because it's such an effective tactic for prosecutors—and because courts aren't stopping them—it makes sense that more and more are using it, as our research confirms. Over the last decade in particular, we've seen a dramatic increase. There are a number of reasons for this expansion, including the role of digital and social media, the formal ways that police and prosecutors have enshrined the practice, and changes in the legal and political landscape post-9/11. But one of the most worrying is that the basic checks and balances that exist in the criminal trial process to ensure that everyone is playing fairly appear to be missing here.

To be clear, while we are focused on the use of rap as evidence in criminal trials, it should also be recognized that rap lyrics are routinely used throughout the criminal justice process. Police are using rap lyrics to identify and arrest suspects. Prosecutors are using them to charge those suspects. Because the stakes are so high for the young men caught up in this—and because rap lyrics make for convincing evidence for jurors—many agree to a plea bargain rather than face a jury that might equate them with the characters in their songs.

Why is rap singled out? There's no single explanation. But without question, race is central here, just as it is in the routine administration of American criminal justice. The statistical outcomes speak loudly on this larger point. Research tells us, for example, that black Americans are more likely than white Americans to be arrested; once arrested, they are more likely to be convicted; and once convicted, they are more likely to face stiff sentences.[33] A number of studies have demonstrated that these disparities exist even when the crimes themselves are the same.

The result? African Americans represent only 13 percent of the U.S. population, yet they represent roughly 38 percent of the state and federal prison populations.[34] When we consider the entire incarcerated population in the United States—to include prisons, local jails, and detention centers—we have roughly 2.3 million people behind bars, the most in the world. Approximately 920,000 of those people are African American, and the vast majority of them are men.[35] To put these numbers into perspective: A black man born in 2001 has a one-in-three chance of being incarcerated. A white man? One in seventeen.[36]

In addition to the numbers, though, the experience of black men in the criminal process has always been qualitatively different than for others. Their cases have never been simply about whether the objective evidence proves beyond a reasonable doubt that they committed a crime. Instead, their race and gender have long been tools for prosecution and punishment. Although criminal court rules today try to minimize this discriminatory treatment, they are often ineffective. And such is the case with rap on trial.

Many of the factors contributing to rap on trial are not new. Society has long viewed black art and expression as a threat and turned to the criminal justice system to control black speech and creative endeavors. From slave drumming and songs to Jim Crow–era ballads, in cabarets and jook joints, and during the civil rights and black nationalist eras, black art and artists have always been criminally regulated. Modern rappers are caught up in this legacy, too, with the use of rap as evidence representing the most current and, in some respects, extreme manifestation of this form of social control.

They are also caught up in the state's long history of invoking racial epithets, narratives, and themes in the courtroom. Prosecutors know that they probably can't get away with using overtly racist language anymore, but it doesn't mean they've given up on playing to the fears and stereotypes that such language evokes. In a criminal justice context—and in mainstream discourse, for that matter—rap has long been a proxy for black (and sometimes Latino) youth culture. Like the word "thug," which is race-neutral on the surface but is almost always used to refer to black men in pejorative ways, rap offers police and prosecutors a convenient way to talk about young men of color while invoking racial stereotypes that would otherwise be unacceptable.

And judges are letting them do it, despite being charged with ensuring that evidence doesn't create unfair prejudice. They simply aren't scrutinizing the evidence for unfairness or ensuring that police experts are appropriately qualified to testify about rap lyrics (which they almost never are). Judges also avoid serious consideration of whether First Amendment constitutional protections should keep lyrical evidence out of court.

Underlying all of these explanations for rap on trial is a basic reality: consistent across historical eras, the criminal justice system, criminal rules, and those who work in the system have demonstrated a willingness to treat black and Latino young men as disposable.

In short, this practice happens because it works, few are aware it's happening, and even fewer are critically challenging it. And it's growing—not only because it is effective and relatively hidden from public view, but also because of the ease with which police and prosecutors can now find the evidence. Dramatic transitions in music format, artist and fan accessibility, and artist profitability have influenced how police and prosecutors find and use rap lyrics. Over time, options for music consumption have evolved from live performances to physical copies to digital formats. Rap evidence has similarly transitioned. When this issue originally burst onto the scene, prosecutors primarily worked with physical evidence, such as defendant-artists' handwritten lyrics in notebooks or recordings on cassette tape, CD, or DVD. Today, the majority of music is consumed via downloading or streaming from the internet.[37] Facebook, YouTube, Spotify, Snapchat, SoundCloud—all of these digital platforms serve as sources for police and prosecutors to find rap evidence.

Another change that has occurred over the years is the music indus-try's expansion from traditional record labels to include independent internet production and distribution platforms. There is no need to wait for a record deal or music station to gain exposure. Artists big and small can directly and efficiently connect with the public by going directly to market through YouTube, Facebook, and SoundCloud. And the artist who develops a large fan base, even if still unknown on a national level, can then leverage that popularity into other mon-eymaking endeavors such as licensing, sponsorships, brand part-nerships, live shows, touring, and festivals. Not only is the industry paying attention, but so are police and prosecutors.

And this becomes the trap of rap on trial. Young adults are making rap music for a number of reasons. It's entertaining. It's creative. It's expressive. But many of the young men we've seen in these cases come from poor neighborhoods with limited opportunities for upward mobility. For them, rap isn't just creative or expressive. It's a potential vocation, and a way out.[38] If they can be punished for trying to rap their way to a better life, then we are witnessing a process that's not just unfair—it's cruel.

Those who have found themselves punished for their art deserve a voice, and we hope this book helps to effect change to that end. How-ever, we want to do it honestly. We are tempted, for example, to offer the typical First Amendment argument, which is dusted off and sent into service whenever speech is under attack. It's the specter of a slip-pery slope, which with rap on trial would go something like this: You might not care about rap music. You might not even like it. But you should still be worried because once we start limiting certain types of speech, we open the door to limiting the kinds of speech you do val-ue. This argument is often used to galvanize support among a diverse group of people by revealing their shared interests and vulnerabilities.

The problem is that we don't believe it, not in this context. Over the last thirty years, even as rap on trial has exploded, we simply have not seen it expand to other art forms. If you're worried, therefore, that country music, with its own history of violent lyrics and violent artists, may be targeted the way rap is, your worries are probably unfounded. The same goes for horror movies or crime novels.

The reason should be obvious. Those are primarily white forms of entertainment, which means they are more or less immune to the kind of judicial attacks that rap music, and the people who create it, endure routinely. So it's important to emphasize that rap on trial is not a First Amendment issue with racial implications. It's a racial issue with First Amendment implications.

That's not just a semantic distinction. We see rap on trial as both a window into the broader racial inequalities that play out in our criminal legal system and a casualty of those inequalities. We don't want to minimize the importance of free expression or the need to protect it; we just want to be clear that we believe rap is being used to punish the people of color who produce it. In our view, meaningful change will come only if we first acknowledge this basic reality.

One final word before moving on.

As is already apparent from this introduction, quotes of actual rap lyrics involved in cases are sprinkled throughout the book. We have quoted the language exactly as it appears in our source material. There may be misspellings, grammatical errors, or slang. The lyrics may be confusing without additional context, definition, or explanation. Yet we have not attempted to offer correction or clarification of these quotes. We have not redacted or edited this language, unless that was the form of the evidence used in court. Virtually all of the lyrics quoted involve language that may be considered offensive by some, including epithets and profanity. We have remained faithful to the original written form as we found it so that readers experience the same lyrics that police, prosecutors, judges, defendants, and jurors worked with in the case. That experience is essential to understanding why this practice is cause for so much concern.

1

Hip Hop: From the Margins to the Mainstream

Understanding how rap on trial began requires a rewind back to the earliest days of hip hop, a social and artistic movement that emerged in response to the dire conditions facing residents in the South Bronx, New York, in the 1970s and 1980s. With much of the Bronx literally up in smoke—the product of disastrous local policy along with nationwide shifts that were gutting urban centers—hip hop emerged as a way to counter the poverty, violence, fear, and despair that residents were forced to endure on a daily basis.

If you visit the South Bronx today, you are likely to see an urban area at the leading edge of full-fledged gentrification, complete with wine bars, upscale coffee shops, and art galleries to complement newly built luxury housing. Real estate executives have even begun referring to the South Bronx as "SoBro," a trendy nickname that evokes the upscale Manhattan neighborhood of SoHo (south of Houston Street).

The South Bronx—the home of hip hop—has come a long way from the burned-out, rubble-strewn area of New York that was one of the most notorious cases of urban decay in United States history. In the 1970s, urban centers across the country underwent unprecedented disinvestment and increasing poverty, but none like the South Bronx. Its fate was due in part to the disastrous decision by city authorities, led by famed city planner Robert Moses, to create a major thoroughfare—the Cross Bronx Expressway—right through the Bronx, destroying homes and communities in the process.

It was also thanks to nationwide shifts in the economy, which led to the widespread suburbanization of manufacturing. Companies had already begun leaving the Bronx in the 1960s, and by the following decade, 40 percent of the manufacturing sector was gone, leaving the South Bronx with 600,000 fewer manufacturing jobs. Incomes dropped to just half of the New York City average and 40 percent of the nationwide average, leaving 40 percent of residents on welfare.[1] Unemployment skyrocketed to 30 percent, with youth unemployment as high as 80 percent.[2] Violent crime, too, went through the roof— by 1970, for example, violent assaults had quadrupled from a decade earlier.[3]

By the mid-1970s, the landscape of the South Bronx became a surreal manifestation of the social and economic devastation faced by its residents, nearly all of them black or Latino. When the sun went down, the area was often still lit, by fires. Between 1970 and 1975, there were more than 68,000 fires, upward of thirty per day.[4] In 1976, that number peaked at a staggering 33,465, roughly a hundred per day. The fires were caused by a variety of factors, some accidental and some more sinister: residents often had to resort to using dangerous space heaters when the heat was either broken or shut off, and combined with faulty wiring, this was a recipe for fires; but many were set intentionally by landlords, who torched their buildings to collect the insurance money.[5] Between 1973 and 1977 alone, thirty thousand fires were set in the South Bronx; on some afternoons, ten or more fires would be set each hour.[6] They became so common that people began to sleep with their shoes on so that they could more easily escape their own burning buildings.

By the end of the decade, the South Bronx had been gutted—between

1970 and 1980, seven census tracts lost more than 97 percent of their buildings to fire and abandonment. Another forty-four tracts lost more than half.[7] With nearly 300,000 people fleeing the area and as many as five thousand abandoned buildings, what was left was a burned-out ghost town, left to packs of wild dogs and residents brave enough to stay or too poor to leave.[8] Jimmy Carter, Pope John Paul II, and Mother Teresa all made trips there to witness the devastation firsthand. In 1980, so did presidential candidate Ronald Reagan, who said he had not "seen anything like this since London after the Blitz," referring to the German bombing of London during World War II.

In the end, though, all anybody seemed to do was watch. The city itself withdrew many of its public services, including police, health workers, and, shockingly, firefighters, leading many to believe city officials were implementing a plan of "malign neglect" in an attempt to depopulate the area.[9] With their homes either crumbling or in flames and nobody interested in helping, residents were literally exposed to an increasingly dangerous and hopeless environment. The physical structures that had once protected them were being destroyed, leaving no place to hide from the crime and chaos caused by the city's apparent withdrawal from the area.

Against this backdrop, street gangs thrived. By the mid-1970s, there were more than a hundred "fighting gangs" across the Bronx, totaling approximately eleven thousand members.[10] Some, like the Black Spades and Savage Skulls, were large, controlling significant amounts of territory, but dozens of smaller gangs sprang up, too, fiercely defending their own areas, sometimes just a few city blocks.

In some ways, these gangs provided a sense of order, creating a power structure that functioned as an alternative to the police, whom many residents didn't trust. But they could also be incredibly violent, preying on local business owners, the elderly, drug addicts, and others. They also preyed on each other. Indeed, just walking through another gang's territory was provocation enough to start a fight, and those fights could escalate into all-out turf wars that spread throughout the Bronx and, at times, the rest of the city. Between the smoldering landscape and pervasive gang violence, the Bronx appeared to be caught in a hopeless cycle of destruction. Many city officials openly opined that it was beyond repair.

But out of this chaos and despair came hip hop. Hip hop is generally defined as an artistic and cultural movement comprised of a number of elements, including graffiti, break dancing, DJing, and eventually rap music. In reality, it was bigger than that; it came to represent a fundamental shift in the way many young people in the Bronx, and across the city, viewed themselves and their community. For many of the city's most marginalized residents, hip hop was a voice, a form of self-expression that was uniquely theirs.

As it began to grow, it also started to undermine street gang culture. Indeed, many gang members started giving up their gang affiliations altogether in the name of this new cultural movement. Probably the most notable and frequently cited example is Afrika Bambaataa, one of the first hip hop DJs, who was a leader in the notorious Black Spades gang. He eventually created the Universal Zulu Nation, a hip hop awareness group of former gang members that was based on a shared political and religious doctrine. For Bambaataa and others, hip hop was an alternative to gang culture, one that drew on the inherent territoriality and competitiveness of gang life but offered a creative outlet instead. Hip hop artists still battled one another, but their battles were metaphorical, fought with turntables, dance moves, and spray paint. Sally Banes, one of the first journalists to document the hip hop movement, made an observation about break dancing that actually applies to hip hop overall: it is "ritual combat that transmutes aggression into art."

Over time, more and more people began identifying with hip hop over gang culture. For example, Savage Skull member Ray Abrahante traded his gang name, 174 Spider, for his graffiti name, BOM5, and also went on to join the Rock Steady Crew, one of the most famous break-dancing, or b-boy, crews in the city. Abrahante's transition from gang member to hip hopper was far from unique; it was the story of the mid- to late 1970s. By then, hip hop was a large-scale movement throughout New York City, one that helped erode a violent gang culture that police and politicians had tried for years to combat. Today, New York boasts that it is America's safest big city. There is no question that hip hop played a part in that transformation.

It also became a vehicle through which many people, primarily young men and women of color, could (re)claim the city as theirs. As acclaimed hip hop scholar Tricia Rose notes, hip hop "gives voice to the tensions and contradictions in the public urban landscape . . . and attempts to seize the shifting urban terrain, to make it work on behalf of the dispossessed."[11] In fact, early hip hop was rooted in the struggle for public space, of "claiming the streets with physical presence."[12]

At hip hop parties, for example—held on public streets, in parks, or at community centers—DJs often battled against each other, taking turns spinning records to see who could win over the crowd. To power their massive sound systems, they would sometimes draw power, illegally, from city streetlights. At these same parties, break-dancing crews would battle for hours until a clear winner emerged. For these dancers, the contested space was the impromptu circle, a patch of ground that served as a virtual stage on which individuals from opposing crews would showcase their techniques. Meanwhile, for graffiti artists the side of a train or the facade of a building became the canvas that, once painted, was marked as belonging to a particular crew or artist—at least until a rival crew came along and, by modifying or defacing the design, laid its own claim to that space.

Although fiercely competitive, hip hop in its earliest moments was intrinsically peaceful. But to a social and political establishment accustomed to silencing voices from the margins, it was highly threatening. Indeed, even in its earliest moments—long before it emerged as a mainstream movement—hip hop drew scrutiny by law enforcement.

Break dancers, for example, were often hard pressed to find practice space because many potential locations were known to be under police surveillance, and even if they did find suitable space, they risked being arrested for disturbing the peace or "attracting undesirable crowds."[13] In some cases, police would actually intervene in breakdancing battles, mistakenly believing the participants were fighting.

And graffiti artists, who drew the ire of city officials once their designs started popping up on trains in wealthy Manhattan neighborhoods, found themselves the targets of "an all-out war on graffiti," with one official describing it as "one of the worst forms of pollution we have to combat."[14] To combat this "pollution," police stepped up enforcement and arrests, and a city teetering on the edge of bankruptcy was somehow able to find $25 million per year (more than $100 million per year in today's dollars) for anti-graffiti efforts.[15]

When these efforts failed to deter graffiti writing, the "war on graffiti" began to resemble an actual war. By the early 1980s, the city began erecting military-style barbed-wire and razor-wire fences around train stations and putting attack dogs behind them (at a cost of an additional $24 million).[16] At the same time, police established a special "vandal squad," which began making thousands of arrests, surveilling high-traffic graffiti areas, and developing an extensive database of known or suspected graffiti artists. It also began monitoring the activities of various crews, interrogating graffiti suspects, and raiding writers' homes.[17] One officer on the squad, describing its methods, said, "We infiltrate. . . . We know where they live, how they live, what schools they go to, where they work: we keep files. We assist various other police departments in naming graffiti artists. We have the biggest graffiti file, I guess, in the world."[18]

In addition to intelligence gathering, brute force was also an option. There are countless stories of graffiti writers being threatened at gunpoint, savagely beaten, and sometimes worse. One of the most notorious examples was the fatal 1983 beating of Michael Stewart, an aspiring artist and model, who was attacked by transit police for allegedly using a marker to scrawl graffiti on a subway station wall. The details of the attack are hair-raising.[19] Stewart was apparently subjected to two separate beatings—one outside the train station, and another outside the police station where he was first taken. Witnesses saw police pounding Stewart with billy clubs while he was writhing on the ground, screaming for help. Despite his pleas, officers kicked him repeatedly, eventually choking him with a nightstick until his screams turned to silence. His arms and legs were finally bound behind his back, at which point witnesses saw the police throw his slender body—which weighed a mere 143 pounds—into a police van. "His body was seen by some to fly through the air before it landed in the van's storage compartment," court documents said.[20] When he arrived at Bellevue Hospital, he was hog-tied and badly bruised, with no pulse. Hospital staff managed to get him breathing again, but they couldn't bring him out of a coma. Thirteen days later, he died in his hospital bed, all because he tagged a subway wall. The police involved were tried and acquitted.

Michael Stewart's case was emblematic of the widespread police brutality faced by people of color in New York City at the time. In fact, the same year he was killed there were congressional hearings held to investigate New York's police conduct, led by Representative John Conyers, chair of the House Subcommittee on Criminal Justice. Conyers held the hearings at the request of black community leaders who called for federal intervention into New York's police practices.[21] Stewart's death was also an early indication of the way authorities in New York and across the country would eventually respond to hip-hop culture.

Intrinsic to the city's war on graffiti, and its subsequent resistance to hip hop, was the deeply rooted fear of black and Latino residents' attempt to spread beyond the boundaries set for them through the de facto segregation that had long characterized American urban centers. Although not inherently threatening or harmful, graffiti provoked a visceral fear among many white citizens that it was just the beginning of a descent into lawlessness. In 1979, well-known sociologist and author Nathan Glazer gave voice to those fears, saying: "While I do not find myself consciously making the connection between the graffiti-makers and the criminals who occasionally rob, rape, assault, and murder passengers, the sense that all are a part of one world of uncontrollable predators seems inescapable."[22]

Glazer's comments offer an important insight into the city's reaction to graffiti and a glimpse at the nationwide reaction to rap music that followed. It wasn't that people found graffiti dangerous in and of itself. Rather, they saw it, and the people who created it, as the leading edge of a more frightening incursion of "uncontrollable predators" who had previously been contained, out of sight, in neighborhoods such as the South Bronx.[23]

The subway made for a particularly poignant battleground. With miles of subterranean tunnels located just beneath the towering buildings of New York, it was a place to grow for early hip hop artists and, at the same time, a symbolic representation of their place in the city's hierarchy. It was an "underground," literally and figuratively, the hidden space that offered protective cover for an art form such as graffiti to flourish.

For centuries, the underground has been an important symbol in black art and culture. Whereas in Western (read: white) traditions the underground represents something foreboding, frightening, or confining, in the black tradition, it often represents freedom, autonomy, and creativity. That's because for as long as there have been black people on American soil, their expression has been contested, marginalized, and punished. One of the keys to survival was keeping it out of view. The "underground," then, represents the spaces and practices that black people have long employed to shield themselves, and their art, from a hostile white America.

By the 1960s and 1970s, however—the era immediately preceding hip hop—many black artists were growing impatient with the idea that they should stay hidden. They wanted to emerge from the underground. This was particularly true of the artists associated with the politically radical Black Arts movement, the self-proclaimed literary wing of the black power movement.

Coming on the heels of the civil rights movement, whose guiding principle was nonviolent disobedience to achieve policy goals, the black power movement took a different approach, asserting the right to self-defense in the face of state-sanctioned racial violence. While the image of beret-wearing Black Panthers armed with rifles is often used to oversimplify the methods and goals of the black power movement—black power was primarily about improving the lives of black Americans, not attacking white people—it is fair to say that many people who identified with black power were far more willing to antagonize the establishment than their civil rights–era predecessors.

Drawing on black power ideology, Black Arts poets took direct aim at America's institutions of power, particularly police. In his frequently anthologized 1969 poem "Black Art," Amiri Baraka, a founding member of the Black Arts movement, writes:

. . . We want "poems that kill."
Assassin poems, Poems that shoot

guns. Poems that wrestle cops into alleys
and take their weapons leaving them dead
with tongues pulled out.[24]

Unlike many of their literary and musical predecessors, Black Arts poets dispensed with coded language and euphemism. They were explicit and provocative, often using violent rhetoric to signal their break from earlier black art forms that they believed were a failure, artistically and politically, because they were too beholden to, and therefore uncritical of, white America.

At the same time these artists were challenging political and artistic institutions, the urban fiction of authors such as Iceberg Slim (real name Robert Beck) and Donald Goines was exploding in popularity. Beck and Goines, the bestselling black authors of their time, sold millions of books that explored the urban underworld, exposing, according to the cover of Goines's bestselling 1971 book *Dopefiend*, "the dark, despair-ridden secret world that few outsiders know about." In works like *Dopefiend* or Iceberg Slim's 1969 novel *Pimp: The Story of My Life*, pimps, hustlers, and drug dealers reigned supreme. With little interest in appearing "respectable" to white audiences, they celebrated a raw form of black masculinity, one that thrived by breaking rules and rejecting mainstream morality. As author Nelson George notes, the pimp figure became a kind of antihero among young black men because his ability to control his environment "has always been viewed as a rare example of black male authority over his domain."[25]

Although they took decidedly different approaches, all of these works shared some important similarities. They rejected white norms, often openly. They focused on the lived experiences of poor and working-class African Americans, depicting the suffering caused by poverty and systemic racism. They elevated black vernacular and black storytelling traditions. And in various ways, they celebrated black strength, even in the most desperate of circumstances.

These were some of the most immediate and influential predecessors of rap music. But it's worth noting that the earliest rap music, made between the late 1970s and mid-1980s and often referred to as "old-school" rap, didn't draw its inspiration from Iceberg Slim novels or Amiri Baraka poems. Old-school lyrics tended to be far less controversial and (with some notable exceptions) more focused on partying and having a good time. The iconic 1982 song "Planet Rock" by Afrika Bambaataa and Soul Sonic Force is a typical example of the lyrics early rappers served up:

> *Everybody just rock it, don't stop it, gotta rock it*
> *Don't stop*
> *Keep tickin' and tockin'*
> *Work it all around the clock*
> *Everybody just rock it, don't stop it.*

By the mid-1980s, however, the rising popularity of rap—combined with the urgency of problems facing urban communities—moved the genre in a decidedly more confrontational and musically complex direction. To this day, many people refer to this period, between the mid-1980s and early 1990s, as rap's "golden age."

During this period, seminal groups such as Public Enemy and Boogie Down Productions on the East Coast and Ice-T and Niggaz Wit Attitudes (N.W.A) on the West Coast were launching direct attacks at institutions of power within the United States. In 1988, two albums in particular—Public Enemy's sophomore album, *It Takes a Nation of Millions to Hold Us Back*, and N.W.A's debut album, *Straight Outta Compton*—marked an important expansion of rap to include overtly political music as well.

While tackling many of the same topics, groups such as Public

Enemy and N.W.A were following decidedly different paths to get there. Public Enemy sounded like a musical extension of the Black Arts—it was sonically jarring and sometimes abrasive, and Chuck D, the group's MC, had a voice that was booming and assertive. At the same time, the group was invoking black nationalism in their rhetoric, drawing on many of the same radical themes found in Black Arts poetry. At the beginning of "Party for Your Right to Fight," for example, a song from *It Takes a Nation of Millions to Hold Us Back,* Chuck D raps about the founding of the Black Panther Party in 1966:

> *Power and equality*
> *And we're out to get it*
> *I know some of you ain't with it*
> *This party started right in '66*
> *With a pro-Black radical mix*

West Coast groups such as N.W.A, on the other hand, were laying the groundwork for "gangsta" rap, a subgenre that, drawing from artists such as Iceberg Slim—the inspiration for rap names like Ice Cube and Ice-T—and 1970s "blaxploitation" films, such as *Dolemite* and *The Mack,* foregrounded the illicit world of pimps, hustlers, and drug dealers. Most West Coast gangsta rappers didn't channel the political rhetoric of black nationalism or embrace Afrocentrism the way groups like Public Enemy did. In fact, they often rejected it outright. For instance, Dr. Dre, one of the members of N.W.A who eventually went solo, raps in his 1992 track "Let Me Ride": "No medallions, dreadlocks, or black fists / It's just that gangsta glare, with gangsta raps / That gangsta shit makes a gangs of snaps." Eazy E, another member of N.W.A who also had a solo career, was a little more blunt when he told *Spin* in a 1990 interview, "Fuck that black power shit: we don't give a fuck."[26]

Gangsta rap brought the underworld into full view, bluntly and unapologetically. At the beginning of "Fuck tha Police," N.W.A's iconic (and controversial) 1998 song, Los Angeles rapper Ice Cube is doing just that when he booms, "Fuck the police, comin' straight from the underground!" No longer content to remain hidden beneath the surface, he is ready to use his voice without fear because, as he says later in the song, he's "got somethin' to say."

Indeed, gangsta rappers in the years to follow had plenty to say as the subgenre became increasingly mainstream and pushed the genre as a whole toward the violent, sexually explicit lyrics that prosecutors would begin to target. But in its earliest days, before it ever showed up in a courtroom, it grew—like hip hop generally—in response to a changing urban environment, this time on the West Coast, nearly three thousand miles from the South Bronx.

Like New York, Los Angeles saw major demographic shifts between 1940 and 1970. Over those three decades, the California city's black population exploded—from 63,744 to more than 500,000—as major industrial companies opened factories in the city, offering the promise of economic stability and opportunity.[27]

By the 1970s, however, Los Angeles witnessed a significant economic decline, driven by many of the same forces that decimated the Bronx. The economy shifted from an industrial and manufacturing base to a service economy. White people began fleeing to the suburbs, and many jobs left with them. Factories started to leave L.A., too, causing a precipitous decline in job opportunities, particularly within heavily black communities such as South Central Los Angeles.

At the same time, President Ronald Reagan had begun the slow process of dismantling the federal government—a process continued by subsequent presidents from both parties. The Reagan administration made major cuts to government-funded housing, training, and education programs, just as cities needed them desperately.[28] As a result, wages and class mobility decreased and income disparity widened. The negative impact of these economic policies demanded that black youth adapt to a new landscape in which their future life prospects were severely diminished.

In Los Angeles, gangs helped fill the void by offering alternative opportunities for members to support themselves socially and financially.[29] By the late 1980s, gang membership grew significantly, with an estimated 70,000 gang members across Los Angeles County, making it the "gang capital of the nation."[30] By the early 1990s, that number had increased dramatically; a 1992 report by the Los Angeles District Attorney's Office proclaimed that "there are 125–130,000 gang members on file in the combined databases for Los Angeles County," with another 20,000 to 25,000 active gang members who had not yet shown up in any gang database.[31] According to the Los Angeles Police Department (LAPD), the racial makeup of gangs in L.A. around this time was 94 percent black and Latino.[32]

Although L.A.'s black and Latino youth found themselves economically marginalized, they nonetheless embraced capitalism. If conventional employment no longer met their needs, they sought out alternatives. By the mid-1980s, the exploding market for crack cocaine—a cheap, smokable form of the drug—presented one such alternative.[33] Without significant start-up costs, small operations and individual freelancers could enter the drug market and make a profit, but so could gangs. According to local law enforcement officials, the Crips and Bloods—L.A.'s most dangerous gangs—had become the main distributors of crack cocaine throughout the western United States.

The resulting crack "epidemic," which spread to urban centers across the country, triggered a particularly harsh response from politicians and law enforcement. They were already waging a "war on drugs"—a phrase introduced by President Nixon in 1971 as he declared drugs to be "public enemy number one"—but the response to the emergence of crack took the drug war to a whole new level.[34]

In the decade that gave birth to gangsta rap, the impact the war on

drugs had on incarceration was startling. With newly enacted mandatory minimum sentences, so-called three-strikes laws, and significant
funding increases for law enforcement and prison construction, mass
incarceration was bearing down not only on Los Angeles but every-
where. In 1985, California's prison population totaled 48,279.[35] By
1995, this number had more than doubled, reaching 131,745.[36] By 2005
it was 168,982.[37] Nationwide, between 1980 and 2005, arrests for drug
crimes tripled, and we witnessed an 1,100 percent increase in drug
offenders in prisons and jails.[38]

Through mass incarceration, black men again became the subject
of gripping government control. In 1990, about one in four black men
between twenty and twenty-nine years was under criminal justice
control. That number rose to one in three in 1995.[39] Before the enact-
ment of federal mandatory minimum sentencing for crack cocaine
offenses, the average federal drug sentence for blacks was 11 percent
higher than whites. By 1990, it was 49 percent higher.[40]

The rise of gangs and crack in Los Angeles contributed not only to
increased incarceration rates locally and statewide but also to intrara-
cial gun violence. In 1992, for example, there were more than eight
hundred gang-related deaths in the city (compared to just seventy in
1974).[41] This increasing violence, along with the hyperaggressive police
response it triggered, became some of the most ubiquitous themes in
rap of that era.

Like many cities, Los Angeles saw violent crime spike as it strug-
gled to contain the crack epidemic. During the 1980s, violent crime in
Los Angeles grew at twice the national rate.[42] For its part, the LAPD
responded by professionalizing and militarizing the force, hiring
Marines as drill instructors and implementing a paramilitary model of policing.[43] The department had already developed a reputation
for aggressive policing, especially in black communities, but under
Daryl Gates, who was chief of the LAPD from 1978 to 1992, the

department doubled down on its hyperaggressive, militaristic approach to policing gangs. Under Gates, the department expanded the use of paramilitary Special Weapons and Tactics (SWAT) units, now commonplace nationwide, and pioneered the use of police helicopters, armored vehicles, and other military-style tools to subdue the population.[44] Mike Davis, in his 1990 book *City of Quartz*, describes Los Angeles during this era as a "carceral city." [45]

One manifestation of this aggressive approach was the creation of Operation Hammer in 1987. A large-scale police effort, Operation Hammer involved massive sweeps, indiscriminate harassment of black and Latino residents, and mass arrests with the aim of cracking down on gang violence. Under Operation Hammer, young black and Latino men who were suspected of being gang members were rounded up and detained routinely, even if they hadn't committed a crime. What's more, many of the people being rounded up by police weren't even gang members. In a single week in April 1988, police stopped nearly 2,500 people on the streets; more than 1,000 turned out to have no gang affiliation.[46] By 1990, police had made 50,000 arrests as a result of Operation Hammer.[47] Routinely police would arrest more than a hundred people at a single time (and sometimes several hundred); most were charged with infractions, and only a small percentage would be charged with serious, felony crimes. The large number of arrests was not the only concern. Under Gates's leadership, unchecked police misconduct and brutality also increased.[48]

Perhaps the most notorious example occurred in 1991, when Rodney King, who was black, was savagely beaten by five white LAPD officers during a routine traffic stop. The beating was documented on video by a bystander and picked up by major news outlets, providing seemingly incontrovertible evidence of police brutality, yet the following year a jury found the officers not guilty of violating King's civil rights. The 1992 L.A. riots that followed were in many ways the predictable consequence of harsh government policies and practices, combined with economic divestment, that had targeted black and Latino communities for decades and had reached a tipping point with the verdict.[49]

By 1992, rap was in full bloom, but it was one of the earliest and most powerful songs—N.W.A's 1988 track "Fuck tha Police"—that could be heard playing across the city as angry residents took to the streets to protest yet another injustice at the hands of police.

Against the backdrop of Los Angeles, gangsta rap became a voice of protest for many, even if it wasn't necessarily protest music in the traditional sense. West Coast gangsta rappers didn't always consider themselves political, but they gleefully flouted convention by celebrating the illicit lifestyle of the gangster and doubling down on stereotypes about hyperviolent, hypersexual black men. In this creative universe of rap, protagonists sometimes killed cops and anyone else who stood in their way, made piles of money selling drugs or robbing people, and had sex with as many women as they wanted. This style of rap was built on larger-than-life characters who were just too big and too badass for the world around them. For them, the rules simply didn't seem to apply.

What made West Coast gangsta rap successful wasn't just its rebelliousness or its ability to tap into America's deep-seated fascination with the outlaw figure. It was also the music itself. Unlike the gritty, raw sounds that often characterized rap coming out of New York, West Coast rap was intentionally laid back, with slow grooves, deep bass, and addictive melodies. Dr. Dre, who went solo after his time with N.W.A, became the key innovator of this musical style, referred to as "G-Funk" because it was heavily influenced by the 1970s funk sounds of artists such as Parliament-Funkadelic.

It was a highly successful formula, one that was making a lot of money—far more than people understood at first. That's because before 1991, the influential *Billboard* charts, which track the nation's bestselling albums, were based upon a deeply flawed system of data collection. Essentially, *Billboard* used a survey method—magazine staff members called record stores around the country and asked store managers what albums had been the top sellers for the week. It was a system rife with inaccuracy. Perhaps the managers had bad memories. Perhaps they had lots of unsold stock of a particular album that they wanted to move by overreporting its success. Or perhaps they were being bribed by major record labels to report high sales of their artists. According to one executive from Tommy Boy records, "In the past, the major labels gave away refrigerators and microwaves to retailers in exchange for store reports."[50]

Then came SoundScan technology, which dispensed with the survey method in favor of point-of-sale tracking. Every time a record was sold and the barcode scanned, it was recorded in a computer database. When *Billboard* began using SoundScan numbers in 1991, the charts changed literally overnight. Shortly after *Billboard* rolled out the SoundScan numbers, N.W.A's second album, *Efil4zaggin*, rocketed to number two on the charts, eventually reaching number one—despite the fact that it had virtually no exposure on radio or television.[51] It was a wake-up to the industry: people were lining up to buy gangsta rap in far greater numbers than the charts had previously recorded. (Groups such as Nirvana and Metallica also turned out to be far more popular than the charts had previously indicated.)

It was just a matter of time before record companies started demanding more and more gangsta rap, which opened doors to the music industry for young adults who had few career options otherwise. But in order to get a foot in the door, they needed to conform to the gangsta image that record companies wanted. Yes, even during gangsta rap's ascendance, there were plenty of rappers who didn't traffic in violent themes. Take Oakland rapper M.C. Hammer, for example. Known, even mocked, for his clean-cut image and lyrics, he released the album *Please Hammer Don't Hurt 'Em* in 1990, and in just over a year it went 10× platinum (10 million records sold). The album eventually became one of the bestselling rap albums of all time. But despite his success, records like his were not seen by record executives as guaranteed profit-makers, so artists who wanted a record deal were often presented with a choice: rap like a gangster or don't rap at all.[52]

In the years after SoundScan was introduced, gangsta rap became more and more mainstream. It was growing on the West Coast with artists such as Snoop Dogg and Tupac Shakur, but by the mid-1990s, New York artists including Wu Tang Clan, Nas, and the Notorious B.I.G. were releasing hit albums that centered on many of the same hardcore themes found in gangsta rap. According to one critic, when Brooklyn rapper Notorious B.I.G. released his debut album, *Ready to Die*, in 1994, it was "the album that reinvented East Coast rap for the gangsta age."[53]

As a result of this resurgence, not to mention growing hip hop scenes in other cities such as Atlanta, Houston, and Chicago, rap's reach was extending far beyond the inner city and into white suburban communities as well. By the mid-1990s, the majority of rap was being purchased by white listeners—by some accounts, more than 70 percent of consumers were white (though these numbers can be difficult to pin down).[54]

White America's response was schizophrenic, which laid the foundation for the trap that we see today with rap on trial. On one hand, white audiences loved the sordid tales many rappers spun. It gave them vicarious participation in communities that in real life they'd visit only if they took the wrong exit off the highway. On the other hand, some white people began to see the music, no longer confined to black communities in New York or Los Angeles, as a threat.

That was certainly the position law enforcement took time and time again. Perhaps the most notorious example was the response to N.W.A's

"Fuck tha Police," which emerged just before gangsta rap exploded as a subgenre. In 1989, in an unprecedented move, Milt Ahlerich, assistant director of the FBI, took exception to N.W.A's lyrics and sent a letter saying so to N.W.A's label, Ruthless Records, and its parent company, Priority Records. Claiming to speak for the law enforcement community as a whole, Ahlerich wrote, "Advocating violence and assault is wrong, and we in the law enforcement community take exception to such action."[55] It is rumored that shortly thereafter the FBI took measures to disrupt the distribution of *Straight Outta Compton* and tried to get N.W.A dropped from Ruthless Records altogether.[56]

Meanwhile, the FBI's response triggered a reaction from police departments across the country intent on interrupting N.W.A's concerts. It worked. In Detroit, for example, police stormed the stage when N.W.A began performing "Fuck tha Police" and later detained the artists outside their hotel. The effect in many other cities was less dramatic: the concerts were simply cancelled due to law enforcement pressure, setting a precedent for police-driven venue resistance to rap that is still commonplace today.[57]

Law enforcement's interest in rap music only grew stronger after N.W.A. For example, artists across the country—including New York rapper LL Cool J, Oakland-based rapper Too Short, and, most famously, Miami rap group 2 Live Crew—were being arrested for performances that authorities regarded as lewd or profane. One of the most notable examples was in 1992, when Ice-T's group Body Count released their song "Cop Killer." In response, local police across the country launched a campaign to force Time Warner, the group's record label, to pull it from the shelves. Sometimes police even took matters into their own hands to stop its distribution. For instance, in Greensboro, North Carolina, local police were so incensed by the song that they threatened to stop responding to emergency calls from a record store that continued to sell it.[58] Soon this kind of fury at the local level went national, and politicians at the highest levels got involved; in 1992 Vice President Dan Quayle called the record "obscene," while President George H. W. Bush railed against record companies that would release a product such as "Cop Killer."

It's important to note that, like Ice Cube, Ice-T intended for his song to serve as social and political commentary. He had no intention of killing police. During the controversy over "Cop Killer," he made that clear, saying, "I'm singing in the first person as a character who is fed up with police brutality. I ain't never killed no cop. . . . If you believe that I'm a cop killer, you believe David Bowie is an astronaut" (a reference to Bowie's song "Space Oddity").[59] In fact, it's worth noting that he went on to play NYPD sergeant Fin Tutuola in *Law and Order: Special Victims Unit*, a role he has held for nearly twenty years, likely due in large part to the visibility and success his career as a rapper lent him.

But the highly inflammatory, confrontational rhetoric that Ice-T and many others adopted made them threats in the eyes of many Americans, and police began taking extraordinary measures to contain them. Just one example: beginning in the mid- to late 1990s, police departments across the country were establishing task forces that were surveilling, and often harassing, hip hop performers who visited their cities.[60] In his book *Decoded*, Grammy Award–winning rapper Jay-Z recounts being followed around New York City by the same "hip hop cop" for seven years and, at one point, being arrested for no other reason than so police could, in his words, "paint the picture of me as a menace to society."[61]

When he considers the reason that rappers are singled out for this type of harassment while other artists aren't, he says, "The difference is obvious, of course: Rappers are young black men telling stories that the police, among others, don't want to hear."[62] It turns out that Jay-Z was wrong. Police (and prosecutors) definitely did want to hear those stories, and they wanted judges and juries to hear them, too.

One of the reasons people seem to be threatened by rap is that they simply don't understand the *art* of rap. They don't know—or refuse to acknowledge—that rap is a sophisticated form of poetry and that artists, even in the most irreverent or rebellious songs, are actually following a complex set of rules and conventions. For DJ Premier, a legendary hip hop producer who has worked with just about all of the big names in rap, hip hop is like a language that listeners have to learn before they can understand what they're hearing. "If you don't know how to listen to it," says Premier, "it doesn't make sense."[63]

This is especially problematic when prosecutors, judges, and juries are presented with rap music as evidence and lack the tools to engage it. Some of the most important features of rap music as an art form— features that can be found in all varieties of rap, gangsta or otherwise— are its emphasis on rhymes and beats, its sophisticated wordplay, its use of exaggeration, and its reliance on repetition.

There's no question that rhyming is at the heart of rap music. Not every line in every song has to rhyme; artists routinely include spoken intros, "outros," or interludes that don't rhyme. But in the end, it's not rap if it doesn't rhyme.

It's also got to have a beat. Like most popular music, rap beats are almost always in 4/4 time, meaning that each musical bar consists of four beats, where each beat is a quarter note long. When discussing poetry, we often talk about this as the meter, with each beat as the foot; for example, Shakespeare wrote in iambic pentameter, meaning that there were five metrical feet per line. In rap, with four beats per bar, the fourth beat marks the end of the bar and therefore the end of the line. Rappers often talk about "spitting sixteen"—that means rapping sixteen bars, or sixteen lines. Usually, but not always, rhymed words fall at the end of the bar, in time with the beat that marks the end of the line.

This all sounds very technical, but as listeners, we are usually quite good at keeping time with the beat. When we clap to the beat of any song in 4/4 time, we generally clap on the second and fourth beat in each line. That means our second clap usually marks the rhyme/beat at the end of the line.

While most of us get this without any explanation, some people don't. In a 2017 tweet, David Simon, creator of the award-winning series *The Wire*, used this rhythmic structure as the basis for an insult aimed at prosecutors in Baltimore who were trying to use rap music as evidence in a criminal case: "In all my years covering crime, I never met a federal prosecutor who didn't clap on the one and the three. Fuck their music criticism."[64] Put more diplomatically, Simon is saying that prosecutors are so bad at understanding music that they don't even get the basic rhythm, so they clap at precisely the wrong time. Without that basic understanding, Simon is suggesting, their analysis of the music is suspect. No argument here. We have seen time and again that prosecutors, along with the police "experts" they call to testify about rap in court, have almost no understanding of the genre, even at the most basic levels.

The broader point is that in rap, there are formal constraints that dictate what an artist can and can't do. In many cases, that means artists choose words specifically because they "fit" within the rules of the genre. Think of a haiku, a poem that consists of three unrhymed lines—the first with five syllables, the second with seven syllables, the third with five syllables. It's one of the most structured poetic forms, and the challenge is twofold: not only must you try to capture the essence of a moment (often the goal of a haiku), but you must do so using words that meet the syllabic requirements exactly.

Rap doesn't impose the same strict limitations. But it does require that rappers rhyme while keeping time with a beat, all the while layering their voice on top of the song's melody. The most skilled MCs not only accomplish this but do so by weaving highly complex rhyming patterns throughout their verses. New York rapper Rakim, who began his career in the late 1980s as one-half of the rap duo Eric B. & Rakim, is widely regarded as one of rap's most important lyrical innovators. During a 2012 interview he gave for the documentary *Something from Nothing: The Art of Rap*, co-produced and directed by Ice-T, he revealed that one of his songwriting techniques involves drawing sixteen dots on a page, one per bar, to map out an entire verse, and then segmenting four bars at a time and graphing out the word/syllable patterns that are possible. If the beat is perfect, says Rakim, "I can take it to the point where there's no other words you can put in that four bars."[65]

Not every rapper follows such a meticulous process. Some take scattered notes on napkins or scraps of paper, and some others—most famously Jay-Z—don't write down their lyrics at all. But in the end, and regardless of their methods, they are constructing rhymes according to a basic set of rules.

Sometimes those rules are not easy to discern. The tricky part about analyzing and interpreting rap music is that rappers employ all the same devices as other poets, including extensive use of symbolism and metaphor. They are highly focused on form, choosing words not only for their meanings and connotations but also for their place in the meter and rhyme scheme of the song.

At the same time, rap is defined by its complex wordplay, evident in its dense slang, coded references, intentional mispronunciations, and sometimes blazing-fast delivery, all of which defy interpretation at every turn. This is often the point in rap. As Jay-Z puts it, "The art of rap is deceptive," noting that rappers lace their lyrics with multiple, unresolved layers of meaning. "Great rap," he says, "retains mystery."[66]

This is a crucial point, especially when it comes to violent rhetoric, which to outside observers, or the average judge or juror, can seem alarming and even dangerous. But as Harvard professor Henry Louis Gates Jr. reminds us, rap "complicates or even rejects literal interpretation."[67]

For example, in rap battles—face-to-face competitions in which rappers often trade antagonistic verses—it is commonplace to use the term "body bag" to describe an opponent's victory over his or her adversary, and extremely violent rhetoric is the norm. In one exchange between battle rappers Loaded Lux and Hollow Da Don—both well known within the battle rap scene, which operates alongside but independent from mainstream rap—Hollow stands just inches away from Loaded Lux and, while making a slicing motion with his hands, raps, "Your death is up, neck get cut, stretch his guts."[68] This is relatively tame by battle rap standards, and while it may seem violent, it's quite the opposite. In rap battles, it's all wordplay.

These kinds of verbal battles occur throughout rap music. Oftentimes rappers aim their lyrics at an imagined opponent; at other times, as in battle rap, artists will go after each other, but using recorded songs rather than in-person performances to do so. These so-called diss tracks have been around as long as rap music has. In one of the most famous, a 2001 song called "Ether," Nas delivers a steady stream of insults and threats at Jay-Z and his Roc-A-Fella label, at one point rapping, "Feel these hot rocks, fellas, put you in a dry spot, fellas / In a pine box with nine shots from my Glock, fellas."

Jay-Z and millions of hip hop fans understood that Nas's threats were part of a tradition in which words are the real ammunition, not bullets. As Andre 3000 of Outkast puts it with rapid-fire delivery: "Put my Glock away, I got a stronger weapon / that never runs out of ammunition so I'm ready for war, okay."

Of course, the wordplay in rap music isn't limited to violent rhetoric. We can hear it in the way rappers bend words to their rhyme scheme, a technique Eminem famously discussed on *60 Minutes* when he demonstrated that, contrary to popular wisdom, plenty of words can rhyme with the word *orange*. His example for Anderson Cooper: "I put my orange *four-inch door hinge* in *storage* and ate *porridge* with *George*."[69] We can also hear it in the words rappers invent, many of them eventually making their way into our everyday lexicon, and even into the *Oxford English Dictionary*. "Twerk," "bling," "jiggy," "shizzle" (as in "fo' shizzle"), "swag," "def," and "phat" are just a handful of examples. "Hip hop" itself is probably the best example.

One of the most creative ways that rappers manipulate language is by imbuing words or phrases with multiple meanings. Jay-Z is one of the masters of this. Take, for instance, the line "I don't half-step on the 'caine" from his song "Hello Brooklyn 2.0," which appeared on his 2007 *American Gangster* album. This line can be interpreted a number of ways at the same time. Perhaps most obviously, especially to hip hop fans, it's a straight-up reference to fellow New York rapper Big Daddy Kane's 1988 song "Ain't No Half-Steppin'." But in Kane's song, "half-stepping" means giving a partial effort, something you don't want to do if you challenge him. So in Jay-Z's lyric, if "'caine" is short for "cocaine," a second meaning is that he doesn't cut or dilute his cocaine; it's pure. Yet another meaning? When he uses a cane to help him walk, he no longer needs to half-step; he can take full strides.

This kind of linguistic fluidity is at the heart of rap music, and it's an important reminder that rap lyrics are meant to be heard, not read. If you choose one spelling over another (like "'caine" versus "cane"), you've stripped away layers of meaning. That's just one of the reasons the music is so vulnerable to misinterpretation. Imagine a prosecutor, judge, or juror trying to untangle the various threads of meaning in lyrics like Jay-Z's. It rarely goes well.

Another hallmark of rap music—one that also lends itself to misinterpretation—is the larger-than-life persona that many rappers adopt. Just as authors create a narrator or actors play a role, rappers create characters, identities that are distinct from their own, often signaled with a stage name. How many people know, for example, that rapper Drake's given name is Aubrey Graham, that Future's is Nayvadius Wilburn, or that Cardi B's is Belcalis Marlenis Almánzar? Very few—including rap fans. That's because even as rappers spin realistic-sounding tales from a first-person perspective, they are ultimately telling stories, not simply rhyming autobiography.

Consider, for instance, rapper Rick Ross, a platinum-selling artist who for years has promoted himself as a drug kingpin with ties to the criminal underworld. In fact, his stage name is taken from the notorious Los Angeles drug trafficker "Freeway" Rick Ross, and in his lyrics, he claims to be tight with the most notorious drug traffickers. In his 2006 song "Hustlin," for instance, he says, "I know Pablo, Noriega / The *real* Noriega, he owe me a hundred favors."

Perhaps the fact that "Pablo" (presumably Pablo Escobar) had been dead since 1993, or that Manuel Noriega had been in prison since 1992, should've raised doubts about the truthfulness of Ross's lyrics. But Ross continued to claim that he "came out of nowhere and just took over the streets," at least until it became public that William Leonard Roberts II (that's his given name) not only attended college, as have many rappers, but at one point worked as a prison guard in Florida. Understandably, he tried to deny his past to protect his "authentic" criminal image, but when employment records and photos of him in a prison guard uniform surfaced on investigative website The Smoking Gun, he came clean.[70] That still hasn't stopped him from rapping—very successfully—and repping a life of crime.

The tendency for rappers to create hyperbolic characters was laid bare in the 2014 federal trial of a Brooklyn, New York, man named Ronald Herron. An aspiring rapper who went by the name Ra Diggs, Herron was on trial for multiple charges (twenty-one in all), including murder and drug trafficking. As part of their case, prosecutors used a number of his violent rap lyrics against him, including lines like "Empty shell casings on the ground / That's man down" and "See if he was smart, he would've shot me in the head / 'Cause I can get you shot from a hospital bed."[71] As part of his defense, he called another Brooklyn rapper with whom he had collaborated, named Lenny Grant, to testify on his behalf. Grant, better known to fans as Uncle Murda, was considerably better-known at the time than Herron, having been on Jay-Z's record label, Roc-A-Fella.

On the stand, Grant testified that many of the lyrics in Herron's songs were either exaggerated or invented. He noted, for example, that despite portraying himself as a wealthy drug kingpin, Herron had to borrow his girlfriend's car because he didn't have his own, sometimes missing recording sessions if he couldn't borrow it. He also testified that Herron was given discounted rates on time in the recording studio because he was broke, and that he used to pick up Herron's tab when they went to clubs. Grant also went further, giving an example of his own use of exaggeration in lyrics. Having once bragged in a lyric that he was shot in the head but refused medical attention, on the stand he came clean, testifying that his head had merely been grazed by a bullet and that he did in fact seek medical attention. Explaining the discrepancy between lyrics and real life, he said, "Sometimes we exaggerate things to sound like the best thing out there."[72] Despite Grant's testimony, Herron was found guilty of all twenty-one counts and was sentenced to life in prison plus 105 years.[73]

Herron's case illustrates one of the trickiest parts of interpreting rap music, which is reconciling its extensive use of metaphor and hyperbole—frequently taken to comical or impossible extremes—with its representations of authenticity. In other words, how do we make sense of a music that, on one hand, gleefully distorts reality but then, on the other hand, claims to be "keepin' it real"?

Whether it's New York rapper KRS-ONE's statement in his 1988 song "My Philosophy" (which was famously sampled by N.W.A) that rap is "not about a salary—it's all about reality," Chuck D's claim in 1997 that rap music is "the black CNN," or any of the countless lyrics in which artists claim to be "keeping it 100"—slang that means 100 percent true or real—there's no shortage of rappers who assure us that their lyrics are, in fact, *real*.[74] And yet, at the same time, some of these same rappers have spent decades explaining that rap music is an art form; they have openly borrowed from poets, novelists, and filmmakers as they create their personas and craft their lyrics; and they take more liberties with reality than acclaimed novelists Gabriel García Márquez or Stephen King.

In the same way, when rappers say they are "spitting truth," a commonly used phrase, they aren't necessarily claiming that everything they rap about is literally true. It's helpful to think about the way we use the word "true." It can mean "in accordance with fact or reality," but it can also mean "loyal or faithful." That second definition is important. For decades, rap has been about being *true*—to your community and to yourself. As Murray Forman demonstrates in his book *The 'Hood Comes First*, this comes through in rappers' constant focus on local geographies—cities, neighborhoods, streets, and landmarks.[75] This allows rappers a chance to represent their communities and, at the same time, establish connections to them. Often, the geographical references in rap lyrics are *true*, meaning that they actually exist, but by naming them, rappers are also being *true* to their communities by shouting them out and putting them on the map, so to speak.

That's not to say that the stories they set in these environments are literally real. The environment becomes a canvas of sorts, on top of which rappers are free to paint whatever they want. As an analogue, consider historical fiction, where authors frequently depict a period or event in history, often taking great pains to create a setting that is historically accurate, even down to the smallest details. This allows the story to feel more real. At the same time, they will add characters, actions, and dialogue that have no connection to history whatsoever. The result is a blend of history and fiction, but without extensive research, most readers would have a very difficult time separating them. For that reason, you wouldn't replace a textbook with a historical novel to teach a high school history class.

Rap works in a similar way. While "keepin' it real" may require rappers to have some knowledge of the world they describe and some connection to it, it doesn't require them to tell true stories. Instead, it requires them to remain true to the art form.

Remaining true to the form often involves representing particular environments, but it also requires that rappers observe the formal characteristics of the genre, and one of the most important is repetition. The earliest hip hop DJs gained recognition for isolating the "break," often a musical or drum solo in the middle of a song, and repeating it over and over. That became an early example of hip hop's use of "looping," which is taking one piece of music (or a sound) and repeating it in a loop as part of a composition. And sampling—using a portion of one sound recording in the creation of another—came to define hip hop's early aesthetic. Before copyright law made the practice prohibitively expensive, groups such as Public Enemy built entire songs from samples of previous recordings. All of this is based on repetition.

Just as repetition is central to rap's structure, it's also central to its lyrics. That's most obvious in the emphasis on rhyming, but it's also clear in the way rappers address similar themes, use a shared albeit ever-changing vocabulary, and draw on one another's work in the creation of their own.[76] To cite just one example, a number of artists have, in the years since 1988, released tracks called "Fuck the Police." These are generally original compositions, but they also draw on, and pay tribute to, the N.W.A original.

That brings up a key distinction in rap: imitating versus "biting." Whereas imitating in order to pay tribute to, or even parody, another artist is both common and acceptable, biting is not. The distinction between them can sometimes be fuzzy, but think of it as the difference between citing a source and plagiarizing it. Professional rappers who bite the lyrics or style from another rapper are often subject to mockery or worse. Short of that, however, imitation is to be expected, especially among amateur rappers, whose artistic development often comes from copying the artists they admire most. That's true of many art forms, no doubt; growth comes from imitation. But unlike with other art forms, imitation in rap can land artists in trouble.

In fact, it happens all the time. In just about every case we've seen, the lyrics by amateur artists that are presented as evidence of wrongdoing have, in fact, appeared many times in songs by more popular artists, often word for word.

Frequently, these aspiring artists are writing all kinds of lyrics, not just violent ones. Some write about their girlfriends. Some write about their mothers. Some write about their cars. But these lyrics don't end up in court. It's only the lyrics about violence or drug dealing that prosecutors cherry-pick and present to jurors. And across the country, there are a number of regional subgenres of rap that include these themes. In the Southeast, for instance, there's so-called trap music—a subgenre of rap that focuses on drug dealing and street life, made popular in the early 2000s by Atlanta rappers such as T.I., Young Jeezy, and Gucci Mane. In Chicago, there's drill, a distinct but related subgenre that became popular after 2010, also characterized by violent, gritty lyrics. On the West Coast, there's Chicano rap, performed by artists of Latin American (usually Mexican) descent, which frequently fuses English and Spanish and regularly features violent, gang-related themes.

These and other subgenres are often distinctive in their sound and their use of regional slang, which varies significantly across the country. But thematically, they are all heavily influenced by early gangsta rap.

And, more to the point, so is rap on trial. Indeed, the use of rap lyrics as evidence tracks closely with the emergence of gangsta rap. As the music gained popularity with listeners across the country, it also gained popularity with police and prosecutors, who saw the potential to use the lyrics in court in order to secure convictions.

2

Rap Enters the Courtroom

August 6, 1991, was a pretty important day in the modern era. It's the day the first website went live on the World Wide Web, a moment with social and technological implications that few people could've anticipated at the time.[1]

For Derek Foster, August 6, 1991, was also important, but for a much different reason. That was the day three judges from the United States Court of Appeals for the Seventh Circuit issued a decision regarding his challenge to his federal criminal conviction.[2] He lost. That's not really surprising. The overwhelming majority of federal criminal defendants are convicted, whether by guilty plea or by trial. And those convicted after a jury trial rarely win their appeals, if they even file one. But for Foster it meant that he was going to finish serving his sentence. There would be no relief for him.

Here are the facts of his case according to the record: Foster took an Amtrak train from Los Angeles to Chicago, where he got off with two suitcases and a blue duffel bag. DEA agents claim they stopped him in the station because he appeared to be struggling to move the suitcases, which kept falling over after being set upright, and he seemed nervous.

When the agents approached him, Foster denied owning the suitcases and said he was helping another passenger by taking them off the train. (Agents were unable to find a passenger matching the description Foster provided.) As Foster was talking to the agents, one of the suitcases fell over, emitting a puff of white dust. Things weren't going well at this point.

Agents searched the suitcases and found a kilogram of cocaine, ten gallons of liquid PCP, and a number of supplies for packing them (including talcum powder, which was the white dust that had escaped the fallen suitcase). They also searched the duffel bag, which Foster did admit was his. Inside they found clothes, train tickets, a beeper, and a notebook containing handwritten lyrics.

Later, during interrogation, Foster admitted that he was a drug mule. He was transporting the suitcases from L.A. to Rockville, Maryland, for a friend who was going to pay him. He said he knew there was "something" in the suitcases, but he didn't know how much. Ultimately, the government charged Foster with possession of cocaine and PCP with intent to distribute.

Foster went to trial, where the only disputed issue was whether Foster knew drugs were in the suitcases. In its case, the government argued that the jury should hear about the lyrics found in the notebook in Foster's duffel bag because it proved Foster was aware that the suitcases contained drugs and was planning to engage in drug distribution. Verbatim, the lyrics were:

> *Key for Key, Pound for pound I'm*
> *the biggest Dope Dealer and I serve*
> *all over town. Rock 4 Rock Self*
> *4 Self. Give me a key let me go*
> *to work more Dollars than your*
> *average business man.*

The judge agreed with the government's reasoning and let a government law enforcement agent—whom the court deemed an expert witness—testify that "key" and "rock" were common words in cocaine trafficking. The court also expressly advised the jurors that the lyrics were not being offered to show that Foster was actually "the biggest dope dealer" or "makes more dollars than the average businessman," but only to show what Foster knew and intended with respect to the drugs. In the end, the jury convicted Foster and the court sentenced him to 151 months of incarceration, followed by a five-year term of supervised release.

Foster appealed, challenging the use of the lyrics alongside other errors. The appellate court rejected his claims. According to the court, the lyrics indicated Foster was familiar with coded drug terminology and drug trafficking, hence he knew the suitcases contained illicit substances.

Foster did point out for the court that rap is "a popular musical style that describes urban life" and "it describes the reality around its author." He also argued that because the lyrics were fictional, artistic expression, they had no or little value as proof of guilt. The appellate court rejected this argument, saying that "in writing about this 'fictional character,' Foster exhibited knowledge of an activity that is far from fictional" and therefore demonstrated his knowledge of the crime. The court also declared that the lyrics did not unduly prejudice the jury against Foster.

At precisely the time rap music was becoming mainstream, the earliest cases in which prosecutors used rap lyrics as criminal evidence emerged. Two of the most influential cases are *United States v. Foster* and *People v. Olguin*. These cases from the 1990s laid the foundation for rap on trial by setting forth the main theories and arguments that prosecutors advanced and courts accepted. Over the next several decades, police and prosecutors would refine and cement the practice, and today we have identified hundreds of rap on trial cases across the nation.

The Opening Act

Both at the time and now, *Foster* may seem like a fairly unremarkable case. But it was important for criminal law and future criminal defendants, because it helped cement the practice of rap on trial. *United States v. Foster* is the earliest published opinion we've identified justifying the use of rap lyrics as criminal evidence.[3] It is the first case whose written opinion discusses lyrics being used at trial, meaning it quotes the lyrics, explains the legal arguments for and against admitting the lyrics, and validates the trial judge's decision to allow them. To date, courts have continued to rely on the reasoning of the *Foster* court.[4]

To be clear, *Foster* may not be the first ever case in which police and prosecutors used rap lyrics as proof of guilt. We believe there are others. In fact, about two months before the *Foster* decision came out, on June 5, 1991, the Iowa Court of Appeals released an opinion in *State v. Deases* mentioning that rap lyrics were used in the trial of the case it was reviewing.[5] But the court, in its decision, did not spend time addressing the lyrics because they were not related to the issues being appealed. If there is a case that precedes *Foster* and *Deases*, it likely did not result in a written opinion that we can find by searching online or in a legal database, and it didn't receive public or media attention that would otherwise bring it to our attention.

It wasn't long after *Foster* that the floodgates started to open, with more and more prosecutors introducing rap as evidence. California became the legal epicenter for this, as law enforcement began to see the value in using rap lyrics to build cases against alleged gang members. To this day, California is home to more cases involving rap as evidence than any other, due in part to its size, but also because of its aggressive anti-gang measures.

The most important rap on trial case from California was *People v. Olguin*, a 1994 decision that effectively authorized state prosecutors to deploy the tactic against alleged gang members.[6]

According to the written opinion of the appeals court, in March 1992, Cesar Javier Olguin used spray paint to lay claim for the Southside gang to an intersection near his home in Santa Ana, California. Sometime later, Olguin's graffiti marking was crossed out and replaced with a marking for the defunct Shelley Street gang. Olguin considered this a sign of disrespect and a challenge. He figured a former Shelley Street gang member must have crossed out his marking.

Olguin, Francisco Calderon Mora, and another Southside gang member agreed to go find out who covered the Southside mark. Olguin armed himself with a loaded handgun. Near the intersection in question, the three encountered Eugene Hernandez, who denied covering the marking but said his cousin, John Ramirez, had. As the three were leaving the intersection, Ramirez appeared and followed them, yelling, "Shelley Street." Olguin and Mora responded by turning back toward Ramirez with shouts of "Southside." After several seconds of yelling about whose territory it was, Mora punched Ramirez in the face, knocking him to the ground. When Ramirez got up and walked toward the group, Olguin pulled his gun and shot Ramirez once in the chest, killing him.

Olguin and Mora were jointly tried. Officer Terry Zlateff, the lead investigator on the case, testified as an expert for the government about rap lyrics found in Mora's home three weeks after the shooting. Zlateff read the lyrics to the jury and interpreted them, claiming they tended to show Mora's loyalty to the Southside gang. The lyrics that Zlateff read include lines such as:

> Well my name is Vamp and Im here to say that I rapp into the
>   beat and I do it this way
> what Im saying is that Mocos ain't nada you fuck with me and
>   Ill turn you into cause Im
> frome a gang that has respect not like the Mecos they think
>   you're dead

Special Introductions frome the South Side Gang. We ware
 born and raised in Santana
when we see that Chacha Quintana Ima shootin in the head
 make him jump like a rana
just to let him know whose controling Santana.
When I walk out my door I have to pack my forty four. R.I.P.
 there a bunch of punks
They will get beat were the South Side Trooper were number 1.

Both were convicted and appealed, challenging the admissibility of the lyrics, along with other issues. Mora argued the government had not done enough to prove the lyrics were written by him as opposed to someone else and that the lyrics might lead the jury to believe he was a bad person. In an effort to shift all responsibility to Mora, Olguin argued Mora wrote the lyrics and they were his confessions, not Olguin's.

Although Mora's name was not on the handwritten paper containing the lyrics, the appellate court concluded that the lyrics were attributable to Mora. The first lyric referenced "Vamp," Mora's gang moniker. The second lyric referenced "Franky," a possible nickname for Francisco, Mora's first name. Both lyrics referenced Southside gang membership. And the second lyric referred to DJing, Mora's part-time job. The court then stated the lyrics "demonstrated his membership in Southside, his loyalty to it, his familiarity with gang culture, and, inferentially, his motive and intent on the day of the killing. The trial court properly admitted them, carefully limiting them to those purposes."

With respect to Mora's claim that the lyrics could improperly influence the jury because they contained violent content, the appeals court deferred to the trial judge's authority and deemed the lyrics important to proving Mora was in a gang and that the killing was gang related.

As for Olguin, the court concluded that because the lyrics were used against Mora alone (the jury was instructed not to use them against Olguin), Olguin's challenge was without merit.

The *Olguin* decision does a lot of things, but most important for our purposes, it establishes that generic lyrics allegedly discussing gang ethos and violence—but not referencing the charged gang-related crime—can be used to prove a person's criminal mind-set and affiliation with a gang. This is of great concern both because it relies on the assumption that rap artists—unlike other artists—are incapable of separating their music from their real lives and because it ignores the likelihood that jurors' preexisting negative feelings about gangs and criminals will affect how they evaluate the evidence.

The government's ability to use rap lyrics as evidence was dramatically expanded as a result of *Olguin*. And throughout the 1990s, as rap became more commercially successful nationwide, prosecutors—with the help of willing judges—continued to expand the contexts in which rap music could be introduced to prove their cases. It was no longer just lyrics written by the defendant. It was also karaoke performances or remakes of original compositions. They even made the case for rap music playing in the background.

In *Foster* and *Olguin*, the defendants being tried presumably wrote original lyrics. By the end of the decade, however, courts also permitted the use of rap lyrics when defendants were clearly remaking, rewriting, or reciting the songs and lyrics of another.

For example, twenty-three-year-old Ishmail Spraggins was charged in Illinois with first-degree murder and aggravated kidnapping for his alleged involvement in the December 1994 killing of Hector Muriel.[7] At trial, Spraggins's pretrial cellmate testified that Spraggins admitted to him how the killing took place and why he wanted to kill the victim. He also testified that Spraggins quoted a popular rap song—"Hand of the Dead Body" by Houston rapper Scarface—in a way that expressed his desire to kill one of the government's witnesses. The lyric, according to his cellmate, was "Nigger don't believe that song / That nigger's wrong / Gangsters don't live that long." Apparently Spraggins substituted the word "snitches" for "gangsters."

The prosecutor argued that Spraggins's cellmate's testimony proved Spraggins was the killer. After his conviction, Spraggins appealed, arguing the prosecutor should not have questioned the witness regarding the song lyrics or argued during closing that those lyrics were evidence of consciousness of guilt. The appellate court *did* find that the trial court erred by letting the evidence in, but because the defendant didn't make an issue of it earlier, he had effectively waived his right to challenge it later.

So a defendant who writes or sings rap music can find it used against him. But what if he just listens to it as background music? Is rap music admissible in that situation? Unfortunately, the answer is yes.

In 1996 an Arkansas jury convicted Antonio Britt of first-degree murder, attempted first-degree murder, aggravated robbery, and kidnapping.[8] The jury concluded that in April 1995, Britt encouraged an accomplice to shoot two people who were looking to buy drugs from them. At trial, over the defendant's objection, the court allowed the government to introduce a tape recording of a song that was reportedly playing in the background during the crime. In particular, one of the lyrics was "Snatch 'em, slam 'em in the trunk, f**k 'em, kill 'em, dump 'em, we don't give a f**k." The victims had been shoved in the trunk of the defendants' car during the crime, and the song allegedly corroborated the manner of the killing and reflected the killer's intent. Reviewing the conviction, the appellate court concluded that because the lyrics depicted actions similar to those taken by Britt and his accomplices, they were admissible.

The 1990s also saw cases in which the lyrics were introduced when a defendant dared to proclaim his innocence on the stand. When defendants went beyond simply questioning the government's case to offering their own evidence of innocence, prosecutors seized the opportunity to challenge them using their connection to rap music.

By the end of the 1990s, as rap music reached unimaginable commercial heights, rap on trial had become a standard practice. It was solid gold for prosecutors, who found that it was an easy sell in the criminal courtroom and so continued to look for new and creative ways to use it. They were rewarded for their dedication. In this ten-year span, their efforts laid a legal foundation that has withstood repeated challenges, allowing it to spread virtually unchecked in the following decades.

Not only was it unchecked, but by the mid-2000s, this prosecutorial approach—rap on trial—had become pervasive nationwide. The vast majority of cases we've identified come from 2005 onward.

Among these was a new type of rap prosecution: threats cases. These cases are different from most others that use rap lyrics to allege a defendant's role in a crime. In threats cases, the lyrics themselves are punished as "true threats."

These cases gained traction thanks to antiterrorism efforts that were expanded at the state level after the terrorist attacks on September 11, 2001. In the wake of the attacks, and the subsequent federal PATRIOT Act, which provided for the detection, investigation, and prosecution of terrorist acts, dozens of states rushed to adopt their own antiterrorism laws. Seen at the time as largely symbolic attempts to combat terrorism, these laws were often broad in their scope, vaguely defined, and carried stiff sentences, giving prosecutors a great deal of discretion in deciding when to use these potentially powerful tools. State laws generally went much further in defining "terrorism" than federal law did.[9]

In Illinois, for instance, a "terrorist act" or "act of terrorism" can be defined as "any act that is intended to cause or create a risk and does cause or create a risk of death or great bodily harm to one or more persons."[10] With no meaningful boundaries, a definition like this creates opportunities for law enforcement officials to investigate and charge just about anything as terrorist, including domestic violence or involvement in a gang, and they have taken full advantage of it.[11]

Given prosecutors' continued expansion of rap on trial, it's no surprise that they've applied these antiterror laws to rap artists. One such case involved an aspiring rapper and student at Southern Illinois University named Olutosin Oduwole.[12] In 2007, authorities found his abandoned car on the Edwardsville campus, where it had apparently run out of gas. They searched the car and found a crumpled piece of paper stuffed between the seats on which Oduwole had scribbled some rhymed lyrics, along with, "If this account doesn't reach $50,000 in the next 7 days then a murderous rampage similar to the VT shooting will occur at another prestigious highly populated university. THIS IS NOT A JOKE!" Police interpreted this as attempting to communicate a terroristic threat under the Illinois statute, which Oduwole was eventually charged with violating.

Like many rappers, Oduwole took compulsive notes when he had song ideas. In fact, at trial a witness testified that Oduwole "came up with the idea for the Virginia Tech rap lyrics while they watched an episode of 'Law and Order.'"[13] There was ample evidence that his note was consistent with other notes and lyrics found throughout his many song notebooks (almost two thousand pages' worth).[14] It was also clear that Oduwole hadn't tried to *communicate* the message to anyone. Nevertheless, the all-white jury convicted the twenty-six-year-old Oduwole, who is black, in 2011, and he was later sentenced to five years in prison. That conviction was eventually overturned, but not before Oduwole spent more than a year behind bars. And in the years since his case, we've seen other threats cases in which defendants weren't so lucky.

To date, we've identified more than five hundred cases involving rap as evidence. But we can also say with confidence that the true number is virtually unknowable given the data collection limitations of today. There is no single resource one can turn to in order to answer this question. You cannot simply pose a query to Google and be given an answer. Criminal court records and proceedings are generally public, but the overwhelming majority of criminal cases do not receive media coverage and the public proceedings and records are not observed. Legal databases, while quite extensive, only capture a small portion of the federal and state criminal case dockets, for a number of reasons. Judges do not issue written opinions on every issue in every case. And even when jurisdictions do make records publicly available, databases do not necessarily collect all the information. This is especially true of indictment proceedings, which are often sealed. The same goes for juvenile court records.

Although we haven't uncovered anything like the full range of cases nationwide, the information we do have is striking and of deep concern. The rap-on-trial tactic is not limited to a handful of jurisdictions or prosecutors. It is prevalent among prosecutors nationwide. We have searched for cases involving state crimes and cases involving federal offenses. We have identified cases in nearly every state and the District of Columbia.[15] The states with the most are California (easily), along with Florida, Louisiana, New York, and Pennsylvania.

By now it should come as no surprise that many of the cases we have studied concern homicide, assault, robbery, firearms, drugs, or gang charges. It follows because to make their cases police and prosecutors often rely on rap lyrics that emphasize these same themes, imagery, and figurative language relating to violence, drugs, guns, and gangs.

With serious charges come serious penalties. In most of the homicide cases we have identified, the defendants face the prospect of sentences as lengthy as twenty-five years to life, and in a smaller but still significant percentage of cases the possible sentence is life without parole. In nearly thirty cases that we've identified, prosecutors sought the death penalty.

And prosecutors have been able to eat their cake and have it too when using rap lyrics in support of death sentences. The rules of evidence that apply to the guilt phase of a trial are different from those that apply during the sentencing phase, when prosecutors (and the defense) are permitted to introduce evidence of the defendant's character. Prosecutors use rap lyrics to show that defendants have bad characters and by nature are hyperviolent criminals who need to be permanently removed from society. When arguing for the harshest of sentences, prosecutors rely on the lyrics to paint defendants as future dangers or to argue that they are depraved or incapable of rehabilitation and should therefore be executed.

Maddeningly, though, prosecutors get away with advancing contrary arguments. On one hand, prosecutors often argue that rap lyrics can be interpreted literally—that the lyrics present factually accurate scenarios that prove the defendant's guilt or demonstrate he is beyond rehabilitation. But in at least one case, prosecutors mixed it up, using lyrics to claim that a defendant, a man named Ronnie Fuston, was quite capable and of sound mind to be executed. In 2017, after being convicted of homicide in Oklahoma City, he faced a capital sentencing hearing in which his defense counsel argued to the jury that he should not be sentenced to death because he was low-functioning (according to at least one IQ test, he was "mentally retarded" under Oklahoma guidelines) and had been abused as a child. The prosecutor rebutted, claiming that Fuston's crafting of rap lyrics demonstrated his intelligence and, therefore, that he should be eligible for execution.

Fuston's was a galling case. His lyrics were standard-fare rap, imitative of celebrated rappers such as Tupac Shakur, Lil Wayne, and Gucci Mane, referring to guns and drugs, among other things. And they weren't directly related to the crime he was found guilty of committing. It's doubtful that the prosecutor really believed the lyrics demonstrated his intelligence. It's more likely that he just wanted the jurors to hear the lyrics before they decided Fuston's fate. They sentenced him to death.

Ronnie Fuston is a typical defendant in rap on trial cases: he is a young black man. The cases we have studied tell us that the practice of using rap in court is highly raced and gendered. The targets are primarily black men, followed closely by Latino men. Typically they are between eighteen and twenty-five years of age. Surely that isn't surprising. It follows general trends in criminal justice which show that young men of color are disproportionately targeted, arrested, convicted, and sentenced to harsher penalties than their white counterparts.

Very few cases involving white defendants—just 1 or 2 percent of the total—have made their way onto our radar. Interestingly, most of them have been threats cases.[16] Even less common are female defendants. To date, we have identified fewer than five cases in which female defendants have had rap lyrics used against them.

One case we've identified is a true rarity—it involves a white woman named Elsebeth Baumgartner. In 2006, Baumgartner pleaded no contest in an Ohio court to ten counts of intimidation and two counts of retaliation. The court found her guilty of seven counts of intimidation and two counts of retaliation, and overall sentenced her to eight years' incarceration.

According to the indictments, Baumgartner was alleged to have intimidated a retired civil court judge who presided over cases in which she was a party (she also happened to be an attorney) by sending emails to the judge accusing him of wrongdoing and emails containing materially false information to the judge's grown children. Baumgartner also allegedly retaliated against and intimidated a witness and the witness's wife for serving as prosecution witnesses in Baumgartner's trial for intimidating the judge. That retaliation took the form of rap lyrics that she posted online, which were an almost verbatim copy of Eminem's song "Soldier." Only a few words were changed.[17] She replaced a name with the name of the wife (Mandy) and substituted a local bar's name for a place name in the song.[18] Allegedly the song posting, combined with Baumgartner's other actions, caused the couple to be in fear for their lives, and they fled the state for a period of time.

Baumgartner appealed her convictions. With respect to the posted rap lyrics, she argued that the First Amendment protected her posting because it was artistic speech rather than a true threat.[19] The appellate court disagreed and upheld her conviction.

Her case is potentially important because it illustrates that threats cases do appear to ensnare white defendants. The question is why. It could suggest that we are witnessing the proverbial slippery slope, where laws intended to curb one kind of speech (or, more accurately, speaker) are then applied more broadly. In other words, a practice such as rap on trial, which targets young men of color, may open the door for prosecutors to use it in other instances. That is certainly possible. But so far, threats cases are still a small percentage of cases overall, and white defendants are a small percentage of those. Right now, there's not enough data to tell us anything about the future for white defendants.

It is worth noting a couple of things about race here. First, we believe that even in cases involving white defendants, race is still operative. Rap music primes certain stereotypes about young black men. The fact that the lyrics may have been written or uttered by a white person doesn't change that. If anything, we believe it's possible that jurors would be willing to punish a white defendant for "crossing over" and embracing black culture, even though rap now can comfortably be labeled a part of popular culture.

It's also worth noting that threats cases—which do seem more likely to involve white defendants—are qualitatively different. Most important, they often carry with them far lighter sentences than, say, drug trafficking or armed robbery, never mind murder. What's more, they frequently involve a conscious decision to antagonize a particular person. In most of the threats cases we've seen or worked on, people are charged for naming specific individuals (usually authority figures) or institutions in their lyrics and directing threatening rhetoric at them.

Don't get us wrong. We think lyrics like this should generally be protected from prosecution. But there is an element of choice involved that is different from most of the stories in this book, where young men are writing and performing rap music, unaware that the authorities are paying attention or that their lyrics could be considered criminal. If you cite a Rick Ross lyric about shooting people who mess with you, or even threaten a rival artist in a rap battle, that's very different from choosing a police officer or school principal in your community and, in rhymed form, saying you're going to shoot her.

Again, we think that such lyrics should generally be permitted, however offensive they may be. But it does make sense that white people would get caught up in threats cases where they were knowingly challenging authority figures. Because they've never been afraid of the police the way blacks and Latinos have, they may be less concerned about antagonizing them.

Over the years, as we have described this phenomenon, we have routinely been asked: "Why? Why did criminal prosecutors begin to use rap in criminal cases during the 1990s, almost two decades after the art form was first innovated? And why haven't courts shut this down since then?"

We suspect that the emergence of the practice paralleled the bicoastal growth of rap, largely performed by black and Latino young men— the same young men who were frequent targets of the wars on drugs and gangs. Prosecutors not only search for evidence, in whatever form, to prove their cases, but also look for a story that best fits the evidence and resonates with jurors. Thus, prosecutors latched onto the fictional reality of rap to use in prosecuting crimes because they often painted a narrative that society—jurors—would more easily accept and believe: violent, criminal black and Latino young men. In doing so, they significantly minimized or outright denied any artistic, creative, or entertaining aspects of the music. Judges, who are tasked with acting as gatekeepers for criminal evidence, neglected to rigorously evaluate the evidence and the arguments against admission of these lyrics. Admission of the evidence became a foregone conclusion.

We need safeguards to end this practice. In reality, the law already provides a number of mechanisms that *should* prevent rap from being used as evidence. The problem is that prosecutors and judges appear to have carved out an exception for rap music, effectively putting their thumb on the scales of justice when aspiring rappers enter the courtroom.

3

Lyrics, Stereotypes, and Bias

On August 24, 2009, twenty-five-year-old Sequoyah Hawkins was walking down Marietta Avenue in Lancaster, Pennsylvania, when he saw his girlfriend involved in a verbal altercation with three men he knew. Hawkins intervened, getting into a scuffle with one of the men in the process, and then began to walk away.

The man he fought with followed him across the street, attempting to defuse the situation, but then the two other men came over to settle the score. One of them struck Hawkins, and in response Hawkins drew a knife from his pants and stabbed the man in the neck, killing him. Hawkins fled the scene and the area, but he was apprehended a few months later and charged with homicide.[1]

At trial, Hawkins testified on his own behalf, arguing that he had acted in self-defense. He feared for his life, he said, as he was surrounded by three men (at least two of them were armed, he claimed, but ditched their weapons). After he was punched, he stabbed wildly at the man who hit him. It was a "reflex," he said. He did not mean to strike him in the neck or to kill him.

He went on to testify that he tried to avoid violence wherever possible and that fighting was not really in his character:

> I just seen a lot of—a lot of things and—and been around a
> lot of things. And from my knowledge of how things work,

> I try to avoid situations as much as possible . . . If some-
> body's fighting or something's going on, I don't run to the
> fight to see what's going on. It's just certain things I do, just
> growing up in the city, that I was able to survive growing
> up by doing these things.

He also testified that the man who struck him was a member of the Bloods gang, known for violence in his neighborhood, which only increased his sense of fear and, in his mind, the justification for self-defense.

Defense attorneys rarely allow their clients to testify at trial. To someone outside the legal system, that may seem counterintuitive. After all, if the defendant is innocent, what does he have to hide? Doesn't he want to set the record straight? In many cases, defendants *do* want to testify. The problem is that testifying opens them up to cross-examination, where prosecutors will try to expose inconsistencies in their story or ask questions that are intended to upset or frustrate them. If the defendant gets rattled and gets his facts wrong—or, worse, lashes out at a prosecutor who's intentionally trying to get under his skin—a jury is likely to hold that against him. Taking the stand is a risk.

Sequoyah Hawkins believed it was a risk worth taking. The stabbing had been recorded by security cameras, and the footage was shown to the jury repeatedly throughout the trial. It made sense that Hawkins would want to provide context for what the jurors were seeing, particularly because he was trying to explain how his actions amounted to self-defense. But in testifying that he was generally a peaceful, nonviolent person, he (perhaps unknowingly) opened up the chance for prosecutors to introduce a new piece of evidence: a rap music video.

In the course of their investigation, authorities discovered a rap video featuring Hawkins. It had nothing to do with the crime he was

accused of—no mention of the victim, no mention of a knife or stabbing, no mention of animosity toward anyone involved. Instead, it featured Hawkins delivering lyrics like these:

> *I have a gun up in your face, screaming take off . . .*
> *4-5 with the safety off, right where your face be, dog . . .*
> *I pull a pistol and put it to your temple,*
> *I watch your brains pop your top like pus from a pimple . . .*
> *Fucking with me and I'm gon[n]a have to kill your ass . . .*
> *blast the mag, your gone [sic] need a plastic bag . . .*
> *sit back and laugh, just watch your gasp, you gonna take your*
> *   last breath.*

A rap song about shooting someone in the head would seem irrelevant
in a case where nobody got shot, but because Hawkins had testified
that he was a nonviolent person, prosecutors wanted to introduce the
video to rebut his testimony. In other words, because he *performed* a
song about violence—a song Hawkins said he didn't even write the lyrics to—prosecutors argued that it demonstrated his propensity toward
actual violence. And in a decision that was equal parts ridiculous and
frightening, the court agreed. The rap video was admitted and shown
to the jury. Hawkins was found guilty of voluntary manslaughter and
sentenced to eight to twenty years in prison.

The most basic premise of evidence law is that only evidence *relevant* to a case can be presented in court; evidence that is not relevant
cannot be considered. As is common nationwide, relevant evidence is
defined as "having any tendency to make the existence of any fact that
is of consequence to the determination of the action more probable
or less probable than it would be without the evidence."[2] In essence,
this relevance standard requires that the evidence be admitted only if
it is some proof, whether direct or indirect and however minimal, of
the crime(s) the defendant is being accused of. Take Hawkins's case.

Let's say, hypothetically, that Hawkins had been convicted years earlier of selling marijuana and prosecutors wanted to introduce evidence of that during his homicide trial. Unless they were arguing that his drug-dealing past was somehow related to the stabbing, prosecutors probably wouldn't be allowed to talk about it. It wouldn't be relevant to the charges, and a judge cannot admit evidence that is not relevant. In the same vein, the rap video that Hawkins appeared in would also generally not be relevant to proving the homicide charge.

But the relevance standard is pretty easy to meet, and there are many avenues prosecutors can rely upon to argue relevance, even if the evidence is just barely helpful to proving the case. In some cases, prosecutors claim lyrics are express confessions of the charged crime. This was the case for Alex Medina, the Ventura, California, teen whose lyrics were depicted by the government as autobiographical confessions to murder, the charge he faced. In other cases, prosecutors rely on an evidence rule allowing them to argue that the lyrics indirectly prove the defendant's intent to commit the crime, demonstrate his knowledge or ability to commit the crime, or reveal his motive for committing the crime. Depending on jurisdiction, this is known as the "other acts," "prior bad acts," or "prior acts" rule. This rule was relied upon in *Foster* and *Olguin*, those early cases laying the foundation for rap on trial. In *Foster*, the defendant's lyrics used drug terminology, so the government offered the lyrics to prove Foster knew about drug distribution. In *Olguin*, the lyrics referred to the victim's alleged gang and the prosecutor used them to show that a gang feud motivated the victim's killing. In the majority of cases we've seen, these rationales or similar ones are used to admit rap lyrics.

But prosecutors did not rely on any of these theories in Hawkins's case. Critically for this case, there is another, less common rule that was used to admit the rap video evidence. Generally, prosecutors are not allowed to introduce evidence relating to a defendant's character, meaning that, with some exceptions, prosecutors are prohibited from arguing that a defendant committed the crime because it was in his nature to do so. Pennsylvania's evidence law mirrors Federal Rule 404, which states, "Evidence of a person's character or character trait is not admissible to prove that on a particular occasion that person acted in accordance with the character or trait."[3] Thus, for example, the government cannot argue that because a defendant is a liar, he committed criminal fraud. In Hawkins's case, let's say that several years prior to the stabbing, Hawkins had been arrested for getting into a fistfight and was charged with assault. Although that might seem relevant (after all, prior incidents of violence might cast doubt on his claim of self-defense), a prosecutor probably wouldn't be allowed to introduce it in the homicide case to show that he has a violent character.

The reason for this ban on so-called character evidence is simple: if you start introducing all kinds of evidence that a defendant is a bad person—or that, because of a prior bad act, he is likely to act that way again—a jury is more likely to find him guilty, even if the facts aren't there. While some people might believe that "once a criminal, always a criminal," that creates one hell of an uphill battle for many defendants. That's why the law takes a different view, at least in theory.

But there is a way around the character evidence prohibition: if the *defendant* makes an issue of his own good character—or the victim's bad character—then the prosecutor is allowed to introduce character evidence to rebut it. So for Hawkins, by testifying that he was generally peaceful and that the victim was a violent gang member, Hawkins opened the door for prosecutors to start attacking his character, and they gladly grabbed the opportunity to admit the rap video.

The way prosecutors used the video reveals one of the underlying assumptions of "rap on trial": that rap music, unlike any other musical genre, somehow reflects the true thoughts, beliefs, and character of the person performing it. Hawkins was in a rap video that had no connection whatsoever to the crime he was accused of; he even denied writing the lyrics. Yet prosecutors said that his rapping violent lyrics in a video was evidence that he wasn't the nonviolent person he claimed to be. The judge agreed.

Consider the implications. Hawkins was portraying a character in a fictional song that, if we believe him, he didn't even write the lyrics to. Because the song was violent in nature, that meant that he was endorsing violence himself, and that endorsement was legitimate evidence of his guilt. If we follow this logic, it becomes mind-boggling how many actors who have played violent characters, singers who have recited violent lyrics, or authors who have written violent novels could find themselves investigated, or possibly convicted, based on their art.

The case is also instructive because it demonstrates the veritable minefield that defendants such as Hawkins have to navigate. If he sits quietly at the defendant's table, he loses his opportunity to defend himself to a jury of his peers, and he runs the risk of looking like a man with something to hide. If, however, he takes the stand and explains why the killing would've been out of character for him, he has just set his own trap. Now the government gets to tell its own story about his character, using evidence that otherwise never would've made it in front of a jury. And in turn the jury could convict him of homicide based mostly on the video despite a lack of evidence proving he is guilty beyond a reasonable doubt of homicide. The jury's logic could be quite simple: if you rap about violence, you must be violent, and guilty.

But evidence rules do provide some protection against this possibility. Another basic rule of evidence is that, although relevant, evidence that might convince jurors to convict because of their emotions—such as bias against a defendant or his characteristics, or anger at or fear of a defendant's past or future behavior—does not have to be admitted. Judges are charged with making sure jurors do not make decisions based on biases or because they are emotionally inflamed by evidence leading them to act irrationally in evaluating a case. Judges have the power to exclude this "unfairly prejudicial" evidence, as it is labeled by Federal Rule 403 and similar state rules. Character evidence is one type of evidence that consistently poses this problem, and so the rules specifically and categorically exclude it, with some exceptions. But judges must be on the lookout for other types of evidence that can also be unfairly prejudicial and warrant exclusion. Rap lyric evidence should be at the top of the list based on what social science tells us about how this evidence biases individuals, including potential jurors. To ensure a fair trial, excluding it is the only reasonable remedy.

Stereotyping Rap(pers)

Rap on trial is a relatively new phenomenon, but it fits within the long-standing, deeply entrenched practice of dehumanizing black men in American courtrooms through the use of racial epithets, tropes, and imagery. Black defendants have been called "nigger," referred to as "King Kong" and "gorilla," and depicted as having above-average strength and sexual desires. Additionally, labeled "dishonest," "scum," and "violent" (particularly against whites), they have been equated with evil, while whites are good. Combined, the perception of rap music and that of black men as dangerous criminals tip the balance in favor of excluding rap lyrics from criminal trials.

The sense that rap music is threatening or dangerous is a reflection of the stereotypes that many people harbor about black people in general—stereotypes that have been used to justify slavery, state-sanctioned discrimination, and, to quote Michelle Alexander, author of *The New Jim Crow*, the warehousing "of a population deemed disposable."[4]

The research on stereotyping is important because it reveals the biases that people have, both explicit and implicit. For our purposes, it's the implicit biases that are most interesting. Yes, there are still plenty of people who knowingly and openly traffic in negative stereotypes about blacks and Latinos. These folks exhibit explicit bias. But implicit bias is far more pervasive (and harder to identify). Implicit bias works at a subconscious level, which the research on stereotyping tries to bring into the open.

It's worth noting that stereotypes are not inherently negative.[5] Essentially, stereotypes are just shortcuts that we use based upon the information we have available about a person or a situation. The problem is that we draw on this information regardless of whether or not it's accurate, and it turns out that when it comes to black men, people tend to draw on a lot of untested or demonstrably inaccurate information.

Studies have shown, for instance, that people are more likely to attribute violent intent to black people compared to white people. For example, a 2002 study asked participants to play a video game with a target subject. Participants were asked, first, to determine whether they thought the subject in the game was armed. If so, they were supposed to shoot that person. Researchers then presented white and black subjects and measured participants' response time. In the end, participants were faster to shoot the armed subject if he was black, and they were faster to decide not to shoot if the unarmed subject was white.[6] This is consistent with other studies showing that people are faster to associate black people with weapons.

Other studies have shown that people's memories can be related to racial stereotypes. In one experiment, researchers presented participants with a series of male names, some more likely to be associated with white/European men (e.g., Frank Smith, Adam McCarthy) and others more likely to be associated with African American men (e.g., Tyrone Washington, Darnell Jones). Participants were told that some names might appear familiar because they appeared in the media, and were then asked to determine which names were associated with criminals versus noncriminals. The study found that participants "remembered" 1.7 times as many black names as criminal versus white names. In fact, none of the names were names of criminals.[7] The results here are consistent with other studies showing that people are more likely to recall details of a crime if it is "stereotype congruent," meaning that it's commonly associated with a specific racial group.

Yet additional studies have shown that racial stereotypes can have a significant impact on defendants when it comes to sentencing. In one study, researchers found that in cases involving white victims, defendants who were seen as more stereotypically black in appearance—based on skin tone, hair, facial features, or whatever features study participants wanted to consider—were more likely to be sentenced to death.[8] This is consistent with other studies that find a link between race and sentencing, such as a 2017 U.S. Sentencing Commission's report finding that African American defendants receive longer sentences than white defendants.[9]

Stereotypical beliefs that black people are threatening, dangerous, and need to be controlled by longer punishments are reflected in people's responses to music—especially rap music. Studies that consider stereotypes and biases about rap music leave little room for doubt that rap music is emotionally inflammatory and therefore very likely to improperly influence a jury. The study that's perhaps the most directly related to rap in the courtroom was conducted by psychologist Stuart Fischoff and published in 1999.[10] Fischoff was retained as an expert witness in a 1992 murder trial, during which prosecutors introduced inflammatory rap lyrics found in the home of the defendant—a young black man named Offord Rollins III—as evidence of his alleged criminal disposition. At the trial, Fischoff testified that Rollins's lyrics were highly imitative of popular rap lyrics at the time and clearly written for commercial and entertainment purposes. As such, according to Fischoff, they were not valuable in determining Rollins's state of mind.

Nevertheless, Rollins was found guilty (by a jury with no black members). It was only thanks to a jury misconduct issue that the conviction was overturned, setting up a second trial in 1995. Here, Rollins's attorney wanted to exclude the lyrics, arguing that they would unfairly prejudice the jury, but he didn't have the evidence he needed to make that argument. So this time, Fischoff was enlisted by Rollins's motivated, resourceful attorney to create a study to determine how possible jurors might perceive or evaluate the personality traits of a rap artist.

Here's how Fischoff designed the study. After recruiting participants, he separated them into four different groups, and he presented each group with biographical information about a hypothetical African American male. (The information was actually taken from Rollins's own biography, but participants didn't know that.) Only some groups were given additional information—specifically, that this hypothetical man was on trial for murder and/or that he was the author of rap lyrics. Participants who were told about the lyrics were also shown samples (which were actually the lyrics being used against Rollins at trial). They included lyrics like this:

> Id die before
> my dick starts to fizz
> pulled it out
> and my head smelled like fish
> rush to the shower
> to wash my dick

Fischoff then asked all participants about their perceptions regarding the young man's personality (for example, whether the young man was caring or uncaring; selfish or unselfish; sexually nonaggressive or sexually aggressive; capable of murder or not capable of murder).

His findings were unexpected. For starters, he found that rap lyrics significantly prejudiced participants. As Fischoff notes, his results suggest that, in the minds of participants, "nice males don't write ugly lyrics and that males who do are definitely not nice."[11] That meant, among other things, that participants who read the lyrics were significantly more likely to think the man was capable of committing murder. What's more—and here's the most surprising part—Fischoff found that exposure to the lyrics evoked a negative reaction that was *more intense than the reaction to being told the young man was on trial for murder.*

The importance of Fischoff's findings cannot be overstated. They suggest, in keeping with other research, that rap lyrics aren't just prejudicial or inflammatory. They are toxic.

When Fischoff's findings were presented to the court in Rollins' second trial, the judge excluded the majority of Rollins' lyrics, including all of the most inflammatory ones. And the result was telling: the jury deadlocked, the prosecutor chose not to pursue a third trial, and Rollins was set free.

Country on Trial?

During his lifetime, country music legend Johnny Cash had his fair share of run-ins with law enforcement and wound up in jail on several occasions. He also wrote lyrics that, if taken literally by a court, could easily have landed him in deep trouble. For example, in "Folsom Prison Blues," released in 1957, Cash sings that he "shot a man in Reno just to watch him die," and in 1962 he released "Delia's Gone," in which he slowly recounts tying a woman named Delia to a chair and then shooting her to death. His final verse would make even a gangsta rapper shudder:

> *So if your woman's devilish*
> *You can let her run*
> *Or you can bring her down and do her*
> *Like Delia got done.*

Notwithstanding lyrics like these, most people understand that no prosecutor would have attempted to use Cash's music to show he committed homicide or had a violent demeanor. After all, these are just songs, and people for the most part don't believe Johnny Cash really did or would have killed anyone, despite his criminal past. And they would be right, at least so far as we can tell. We haven't found any examples where country music, by Cash or anyone else, has been used in a criminal trial the way rap is.

In some ways, that should be something of a surprise. After all, rap and country, while superficially different musical genres, have a natural affinity and share many similarities. Born as distinct genres approximately fifty years apart, both began as outsider or outlaw musical genres. The two often reject artistic and cultural norms and embrace the lives of marginalized folks, whether black or white—the common man, so to speak.[12] And despite their outsider beginnings, over time both have moved from the street to the boardroom. They have become commercially profitable genres and mainstreamed within the music industry.[13] Moreover, not only have their origins as fiercely independent rebels softened, they have begun to blend with each other and with other musical genres. Artists have blended their sounds through collaborations, featuring guest artists on their works, and creating collectives. In 1986, the rap group Run DMC, a staple in the golden age of hip hop, collaborated with legendary rock band Aerosmith to record "Walk this Way." Fast-forward thirty years and in 2018 you can find country music star Carrie Underwood collaborating with longtime rapper Ludacris, or leading pop-country recording artist Taylor Swift partnering with rapper T-Pain. Now you can even find a niche fusion of country and rap known as hick-hop, which originated in the 1990s and took off in the 2000s.[14]

Rap and country also deal with some similar themes. Both speak (at least at times) to sex, drug or alcohol (ab)use, poverty, and certainly violence. Indeed, the murder ballad, which can be traced back centuries, has always had a prominent place in country music thanks to icons such as Johnny Cash, Waylon Jennings, and Willie Nelson as well as many others who are less famous. Murder "ballads" are also common among rappers, especially after the emergence of N.W.A.

There are lots of other commonalities, too—a focus on authenticity, an interest in representing geographies (cities, states, regions), and interestingly, a tendency for artists in each genre to get in trouble with the law.[15]

All of this is to say that because of the many, many similarities between them, you might wonder why, despite our searching, we have not yet uncovered instances of prosecutors using lyrics from country music.

A 1999 study by social psychologist Carrie B. Fried helps explain why.[16] Fried devised an experiment in which she pitted rap against country music. To do this, she presented to two groups of people an identical set of violent lyrics, taken from a song called "Bad Man's Blunder" by the Kingston Trio, a folk/pop band that began recording in the 1950s. The lyrics included passages like this:

Well, early one evening I was roamin' around,
I was feelin' kind of mean, I shot a deputy down.

Strolled along home and I went to bed.
Well, I laid my pistol up under my head.

Fried removed all information related to the song's title, origin, or genre. All that was left were the lyrics. Then one group was told those lyrics came from a country song, while the other was told those exact same lyrics came from a rap song. The participants were then asked to indicate how much they agreed with a series of statements about the song, including these:

"This song promotes violence, riots, and civil unrest."
"This song may be dangerous or harmful to society."
"They should ban such songs entirely."

As Fried hypothesized, responses were significantly more negative when the lyrics were represented as rap, revealing, to quote Fried, that "the same lyrical passage that is acceptable as a country song is dangerous and offensive when identified as a rap song."[17] She emphasizes an important racial dimension, too. Whereas country music is traditionally associated with white performers, rap "primes the negative culturally held stereotype of urban Blacks."[18]

Fried's claims about race are based on more than just this study (published in 1999). In 1996, she conducted a similar study, also revealing bias against rap music.[19] Especially of interest here is that in this earlier study she used the same Kingston Trio lyrics, but in one test she showed groups a picture of the artist instead of telling them the genre of music. Each group got lyrics and a head shot of the person they were told was the artist, and nothing else. One group got a picture of a young black man, while the other got a picture of a young white man. No big surprise here—people's response to the *same* lyrics was significantly more negative when they believed the artist was black.

One last thing about Fried's findings: age is important. In her 1999 study, she found that participants under the age of forty did not have a significantly different response to the lyrics whether they were labeled as rap or country. But among participants over forty—and particularly among participants between forty and fifty-two years of age—the bias was unmistakable (and statistically significant).

For rap on trial, the obvious question that follows is, how old are the people serving on juries? That's not entirely clear, largely because courts don't compile or disseminate that information in uniform ways. But according to one study, which looked at jury pools in nearly eight hundred felony trials in Florida, the average age of jurors was 49.6 years old.[20] If that can be taken as a reasonable approximation of how old juries are, that's really bad news for defendants whose rap lyrics are being used against them.

Some might object that Fried's study is twenty years old, and therefore that the findings are outdated. As noted earlier, though, her experiment was replicated in 2016 by researchers from UC Irvine, who found that what was true in 1999 is still true today. Specifically, they reported that "participants deemed the exact same lyrics to be more offensive, in greater need of regulation, and *more literal* when characterized as rap compared with country."[21] They also found, following Fried, that age played a significant factor, with older people much more likely to find differences between the "rap" and "country" samples.[22]

Metal on Trial?

Heavy metal music, birthed in the late 1960s and early 1970s, has been criticized (often fairly) for being violent, aggressive, dark, depressing, angry, and misogynistic. If you are looking for the grossest, most twisted lyrics you can find, it's a good bet you'll find them in heavy metal, a genre in which nothing—not cannibalism, not animal rape, not devil worship, not serial murder—is off-limits.

As a result, heavy metal has found itself in hot water from time to time. In two well-known cases, heavy metal artists were the target of civil lawsuits brought by parents whose children had committed suicide after listening to their music. The accusations brought against the artists were slightly different. In one case, brought against notorious heavy metal artist Ozzy Osbourne in 1986, parents argued that the lyrics in Osbourne's song "Suicide Solution"—which included lines like "Where to hide? Suicide is the only way out"—pushed their son to take his own life. In another case, a 1990 lawsuit brought against equally infamous heavy metal band Judas Priest accused the group of inserting subliminal messages in their music that encouraged listeners to kill themselves.

These cases were civil, not criminal. The families involved were seeking damages, but nobody was in danger of being incarcerated. Further, both cases were dismissed, sending an early message from the courts that lawsuits like these were not likely to succeed. Finally, the accusations themselves were very different from rap on trial. With Ozzy Osbourne and Judas Priest, nobody was arguing that the artists themselves were committing crimes by living out their lyrics. They were arguing that the lyrics caused listeners to behave in self-destructive ways.

That same approach has occasionally been used in criminal cases as well, with prosecutors using heavy metal (or death metal, an especially graphic subgenre) at trial to explain to jurors what motivated a defendant to engage in criminal, usually violent, behavior. In other cases, defendants themselves have introduced heavy metal music, arguing that it motivated them in some way to engage in criminal behavior. In either scenario, heavy metal, like rap, has the potential to make jurors decide cases based on bias and emotion rather than the evidence.

Nevertheless, while prosecutors have used heavy metal songs and lyrics as evidence in criminal trials, there are noticeable and important differences from the spectacle of rap as evidence. Most important among them is that research has uncovered far fewer of these cases. Next, these cases don't involve law enforcement experts offering their interpretation of the lyrics. And finally, it bears repeating that the defendants in these cases are usually mere listeners, not the authors; the music is being depicted as a bad influence, causing people to do self-destructive things.

That is a crucial point because it reveals a fundamental difference in the way people perceive rock and rap. Between 1985 and 1990—exactly when the Osbourne and Judas Priest cases were happening—sociologist Amy Binder was studying the way rock and rap music were depicted in the mainstream media. Since both genres were being vilified regularly—this was precisely the same timeframe when rap groups like N.W.A and 2 Live Crew were shocking people daily and attracting the attention of government officials—she designed a study to determine if there were any differences in the way each genre was being portrayed.[23]

According to Binder, when writers addressed the negative aspects of rap, they did so in a different way: "Mainstream writers were no longer concerned about the detrimental effects of the graphic music on teenaged listeners, as they had been for heavy metal, but were concerned about the dangers these black youths posed to the society at large." In other words, people saw heavy metal as something that could be harmful to its listeners, while rap could cause its black listeners to hurt others. Binder is explicit about race in her discussion, noting that writers in the mainstream media "constructed images of race and adolescence to tell separate stories of the dangers lurking in the cultural expressions of the two distinct social groups."[24] In those stories, rap music was framed as something that could compel black listeners to hurt white people.

In 2003, Carrie Fried (the same psychology researcher behind the study of rap and country music) set out to test whether Binder's findings would apply to people's perceptions of *fans* of rap versus fans of heavy metal. To do this, she designed an experiment in which participants were given a form that asked them to take a moment and envision either the "typical fan of rap music" or the "typical fan of heavy metal."[25] Participants were then asked to list as many traits as possible about rap fans or heavy metal fans, depending on which form they received.

Fried essentially confirmed what Binder had found. Fans of rap music were more likely to be described as threats to society. This included references to crimes against others, gang activity, and anger or aggression. Heavy metal fans were more likely to be associated with self-destructive behaviors, such as substance abuse or suicide. To summarize her findings, Fried notes that "heavy metal fans were seen as a threat to themselves while rap fans were seen as a threat to others."[26]

Emerging research has only added weight to these findings. A 2018 study, for example, considered people's reactions when presented with lyrics they believed were rap, country, or heavy metal, though the lyrics were the same for everyone—they came from "Bad Man's Blunder," the song from the Fried study.[27] What did the researchers find? This shouldn't come as a surprise:

> It appears that those who write violent "rap" lyrics are more easily associated with crime and violence than those who write identical violent lyrics labeled as different genres. In particular, participants are more likely to assume that a rapper is in a gang, has a criminal record, and is involved in criminal activity than are artists from other music genres, and this is based merely on the genre of the lyrics.

Rightly, the researchers apply their findings to the courtroom, warning judges that they should beware of the negative character inferences jurors might make from rap lyrics and noting that such evidence can be "especially harmful for Black defendants, particularly when it reinforces stereotypes about Black men and criminality."

Collectively, these studies demonstrate the power that individual beliefs about blackness, particularly black masculinity, and rap music may have over jurors deciding the guilt or innocence of a young black male criminal defendant. Consider now that these biases are leveraged and amplified by prosecutors using rap evidence to spin a tale of guilt in which the defendant fits within preconceived notions of black criminality.

Tales of Guilt

Training materials routinely advise trial lawyers of all sorts to tell a coherent story that will resonate with jurors and make sense of the evidence presented to them. This advice is drawn from a rich body of empirical literature.[28] Further, legal doctrine endorses this guidance. The Supreme Court has stated that prosecutors generally must be allowed to control the stories they craft for jurors and may admit evidence for this purpose.[29] In the Court's estimation, jurors may be confused if not presented with a coherent narrative, so much so that the Court warned that if prosecutors couldn't prove their case using their evidence and controlling the narrative, jurors might punish them by acquitting.

A visit to any courtroom during closing arguments of a criminal case provides an opportunity to witness legal storytelling in action. These are not simple short stories. They are fully fleshed out, complete with plots, characters, settings, and motive. The prosecutor's goal is to tell a compelling story that works with the government's evidence, is better than the defendant's story, and "makes sense." The logic follows that jurors will then create their own stories and choose the best among all the versions in order to determine the truth and then guilt.[30]

Although prosecutors are granted narrative control with respect to introduction of evidence and arguments for guilt, they are supposed to do so without racial imagery and racial epithets. Legal doctrine from the Supreme Court seems unambivalent on this point.[31] Nonetheless, research confirms that even into the twenty-first century prosecutors continue to refer to black men using racial imagery, epithets, and stereotypes. And when they do so, courts don't always flag those references as inappropriate.[32]

And while in many instances prosecutors who introduce rap lyrics are not explicitly relying on blatantly biased language or images, the evidence permits them to call black male defendants "thugs," "gangsters," and "gangbangers," which essentially function as euphemisms for black criminals.[33] Or even if prosecutors do not use the language, others in the process may understand the implicit meaning of the evidence and use the terms.

Society trains people—potential jurors—to hold racist predispositions, conscious or unconscious, against young black men and against rap music evidence. Thus, even before a juror has heard any other evidence in a case, the lyrics by themselves raise the potential for unfair prejudice. When coupled with a prosecutor's ability to use admitted lyrics to tell a story of guilt by drawing on stereotypes of black male criminality, surely courts should find it reasonable to exclude the lyrics as unfairly prejudicial so that jurors do not convict for the wrong reasons. But they do not.

Take the case of Blaine Brooks, who was charged with a gang-related murder after his lyrics were introduced as evidence. In May 1999, Pike County, Mississippi, resident Merry Wilson was found dead in her home. It appeared that she had died at least a couple of days earlier in what authorities believed was a struggle that ended in her being stabbed multiple times by a fork.

Despite what many of us would expect based on hour-long television dramas such as *Law & Order*, *NYPD Blue*, and *NCIS*, in which highly competent, dedicated teams of police and prosecutors use every possible high-tech tool at their disposal to solve crimes and bring perpetrators to justice—an alluring narrative that builds confidence in law enforcement capabilities and helps bolster our faith in the logic of the criminal justice system and, consequently, the fairness of its outcomes—the police investigation of Wilson's death was humorously bad. When police arrived on the scene, they entered the house and then accidentally locked themselves out, requiring them to break a window to reenter. On that same day, they saw a car parked in Wilson's carport and observed a handprint on the trunk but chose not to analyze it because it was too dusty. Sometime in the days after police secured the premises, someone broke into that car and went through the glove compartment. Police didn't examine the glove compartment for fingerprints. About three weeks after police discovered that the car had been broken into, the car was stolen and wasn't recovered.

Inside the house, police found evidence of a struggle throughout the house and identified sixteen sets of fingerprints. Near where Wilson's body was found, police also found blood and a piece of jewelry with a strand of hair in it. Two of the fingerprints matched Merry Wilson's, but police were unable to match the others to Wilson (or, for that matter, the man they ultimately charged). The pathologist took scrapings from Wilson's fingernails and sent them to the crime lab, but the sheriff's department never received the results of the tests. The crime scene analyst later testified that they never tested the strand of hair found intertwined in the jewelry. His explanation? He didn't have a sample to compare it with, even though, presumably, he could've requested a sample at any time from the victim's body, or the defendant in the case.

Eventually, police spoke to a woman named Sherry Maxine Hodges Smith, Blaine Brooks's aunt, who initially claimed that she learned about the murder by hearing it over the police scanner. That was a lie; police hadn't relayed any information about the murder over the scanner. So she changed her story and said Towanda Nobles, Brooks's mother and her own half sister, told her that Brooks had admitted to the murder. (If this is difficult to follow, that's because it's hearsay—actually *double* hearsay. One person is attesting to what another person said he or she was told by yet another person.) Nobles, however, denied that her son confessed.

Nevertheless, Brooks was eventually charged in the case, and police continued their string of errors and improprieties. One of them involved an eyewitness. On the day Wilson's body was discovered, a woman named Sandra Graham contacted police and said she had seen a dark-skinned African American man in a truck leaving Wilson's driveway on May 13, which may or may not have been the day Wilson was killed (investigators couldn't tell precisely).

The problem? Brooks is not dark-skinned by anyone's estimation, including Graham's. Perhaps that's why police showed her three photos of Brooks, and nobody else, before conducting two separate lineups that included Brooks without an attorney present. It is unclear why they conducted two lineups, and the record is strangely silent on that. But it seems pretty obvious that despite totally improper coaching (with the three preliminary photos of Brooks), Graham couldn't identify Brooks the first time around.

This is essentially *CSI* meets Monty Python (the famous British comedy group), except it's not funny because prosecutors actually took this case to trial with no physical evidence, a double hearsay confession from a questionable witness, and a totally blown eyewitness identification.

Enter rap music. Just days before the trial began, prosecutors came up with a new theory: that Brooks was in a gang and the murder was gang-related. This is a common tactic that we've seen over and over. Recall that, as a general rule, prosecutors are not supposed to introduce evidence of a defendant's bad character because that might unfairly influence a jury. But if you're a prosecutor and you don't have a case, you really want to get character evidence in front of a jury, so you need a good excuse to do it.

Prosecutors, perhaps disingenuously, advanced a theory of gang involvement. They argued that Brooks was in the Gangster Disciples, a gang founded in the late 1960s in Southside Chicago but whose reach has since gone national. The Gangster Disciples use a three-pronged pitchfork as one of its symbols. Brooks had a tattoo of the Grim Reaper holding a pitchfork, which was one of the ways they established his gang membership. From there, prosecutors argued that Brooks, in the midst of the violent struggle that ended in Wilson's death, paused at a kitchen drawer to select as his murder weapon a carving fork (which had just two prongs) as his "calling card." This was now a gang-related murder. However ridiculous the argument, it was clever because prosecutors could argue that this evidence was being introduced not to show Brooks's bad character but to establish his identity as the killer. The judge bought it.

As Brooks's attorneys would later write, "Defendant's motion to exclude gang and other character evidence was denied, and the flood gates opened." Prosecutors began introducing all kinds of information about gangs and tattoos, but they also read to the jury some rap lyrics that they found at Brooks's house. They included lines like this: "Five shots to a punk, have 'em laying in the trunk. Oh you didn't know, down south we get crunk. Pistol grip pump ah four five to a 30-30 we down an dirty."[34]

The lyrics did not mention the victim. They did not mention gangs. They did not mention stabbing. What's more, Brooks said that he didn't compose the lyrics at all, and prosecutors offered no evidence to refute that—no handwriting analysis, no signatures on the pages, no witnesses who saw him write the lyrics. Nothing. The judge allowed the lyrics anyway. (The fairer approach, though, would have been for the judge to require the government to prove who authored the lyrics, based on rules regarding the authentication of evidence.)

And so in lieu of credible evidence, the jury was flooded with a bunch of gang-related evidence and violent, murderous rap lyrics that had no real connection to the case at all. They returned a verdict of guilty, and Brooks was sentenced to life in prison.

That might seem outrageous, but it speaks to the reason protective rules exist in the first place. If you put highly prejudicial, inflammatory evidence before jurors, they are likely to find guilt even when the evidence is lacking and reasonable doubt is obvious.

And it's not as though Brooks's attorneys were asleep at the wheel. Throughout the trial, they objected vigorously to everything—the questionably obtained identification, the double hearsay "confession," and certainly the rap lyrics. But, as we've come to expect, the judge ruled in favor of prosecutors and allowed the evidence at trial.

What's worse, when Brooks appealed, the Court of Appeals sided with the trial court judge, upholding the conviction. In its ruling, the court sidestepped the rap lyrics altogether. Despite the fact that Brooks's appeal addressed, at length, the reasons the lyrics shouldn't have been introduced, the court decided not to address those arguments at all. Its opinion doesn't even mention rap lyrics.

For most people convicted of a crime, this is as far as their case is likely to go. While they still have recourse, in theory at least, to higher courts, the odds that their cases will be heard at a higher level are slim. The U.S. Supreme Court, for instance, the highest court in the country, agrees to review less than 3 percent of the cases it is asked to decide.

Brooks was lucky. After his appeal was denied by the Court of Appeals, he petitioned the Supreme Court of Mississippi, which agreed to hear the case. The state Supreme Court tore the case apart, finding it to be as bad on legal grounds as a layperson would find it to be on commonsense grounds. It found that the line-up identification was improper and that the hearsay confession never should have been admitted. But unlike the Court of Appeals, it addressed the rap lyrics directly, finding that they never should have been admitted either.

In its 2005 opinion, the court wrote the following:

> The trial court allowed the State to introduce into evidence some rap lyrics presumably written by Brooks which extolled murder. Additionally, the trial court allowed the State to inform the jury that Brooks had been involved in gang activity and that he had a tattoo of the Grim Reaper holding a pitchfork. . . . The State tells us this evidence was not offered to show Brooks's bad character, but rather for the purpose of identity because the victim was stabbed repeatedly in the neck with a meat fork. In other words, the gang follows the devil; the devil uses a pitchfork; the victim was stabbed with a meat fork. . . . The lyrics presumably written by the defendant make no mention of gangs. The lyrics discuss murder by use of a gun, not a fork. . . . [T]he trial court made no attempt on the record to determine whether the probative value of the evidence outweighed the prejudicial harm. Furthermore, we find that, based upon the record before us, the tattoo and gang-related evidence would not have survived a Rule 403 analysis had it been conducted.

In other words, the court decided that the rap lyrics and other gang-related evidence were significantly more likely to bias the jury against the defendant than they were useful in determining guilt. Other high-level courts have reached the same conclusion in rap lyrics cases, including the highest courts in New Jersey (*State v. Skinner*), Massachusetts (*Commonwealth v. Lamory Gray*), and Maryland (*Hannah v. State*). These are important decisions, but they are outliers. Most courts allow the lyrics, despite the mounting scientific evidence that they have very little value in proving guilt and do indeed lead jurors to make bad decisions.

Given the lax attitude toward allowing rap lyrics in courts, you may by now be wondering: What about freedom of speech? Doesn't that prevent the government from using rap music as criminal evidence? After all, *it is* a form of expressive speech with deep artistic roots, and isn't that what the First Amendment protects?

4

What About the First Amendment?

On November 11, 2012, two Pittsburgh, Pennsylvania, police officers pulled over a vehicle driven by a young black man named Leon Ford Jr. for minor traffic violations. During the course of the stop, Ford produced a valid driver's license, a valid vehicle registration, and valid proof of insurance, but police somehow became convinced that he was actually a man named Lamont Ford, a violent gang member. They called a police detective to the scene to help them sort out Ford's identity.

When the detective arrived, the situation quickly escalated. Police directed a now terrified Ford to get out of the vehicle, but when he refused do so, citing his fear, the officers tried to forcibly pull him out of the vehicle. As this was happening, the detective claimed he saw a bulge in Ford's pocket and, believing it was a gun, jumped into the car as it began to drive away. The detective shot Ford five times, causing the car to crash.

Ford was permanently paralyzed from the shooting. He didn't have a gun. And he wasn't the man police claimed he was. The city later settled with Ford for $5.5 million.[1]

Two of Ford's friends, eighteen-year-old Jamal Knox and twenty-one-year-old Rashee Beasley, had their own troubles with Pittsburgh police and decided to speak up about it. Even before Ford was shot, Knox and Beasley, both aspiring rap artists, recorded a song called "Fuck the Police," modeled after N.W.A's iconic song with the same title. Knox and Beasley's version was raw. It named two Pittsburgh police officers directly, both of whom had arrested Knox and Beasley months before Ford's shooting (one of them, Michael Kosko, was involved in Ford's shooting as well). It included lines like "Let's kill these cops cuz they don't do us no good/Pullin' your Glock out cause I live in the hood/You dirty bitches."

After Ford's shooting became public, the video was uploaded to YouTube by a friend of Knox and Beasley's and then linked to Beasley's Facebook account. But police had been secretly monitoring his Facebook account. They quickly spotted the video and charged Knox and Beasley with communicating a terroristic threat, a felony under Pennsylvania law. As is quite common in threats cases, the lawyers for Knox and Beasley raised a First Amendment defense, arguing that the song was protected speech. Their argument was rejected, and although the two young men denied that they intended to harm anyone, the trial judge found them guilty of making terroristic threats and sentenced them to prison.

It is widely known that the First Amendment provides constitutional protections for speech and applies to artistic and creative expression. It might be less known that First Amendment protections also generally extend to inflammatory and offensive language, which makes the First Amendment central to any discussion of rap on trial. But courts consistently fail to apply these First Amendment protections to rap lyrics in criminal trials. And even when the issue is front and center in a case, as it is when a defendant is charged with making a criminal threat, constitutional challenges are quickly rejected.

Pleading the First (Amendment)

The First Amendment to the United States Constitution mandates the following:

Congress shall make no law respecting an establishment of religion, or prohibiting the free exercise thereof; *or abridging the freedom of speech*, or of the press; or the right of the people peaceably to assemble, and to petition the Government for a redress of grievances. [Emphasis added]

Freedom of speech, a bedrock principle that in many ways defines and distinguishes America, is derived *solely* from the handful of words in italics in the preceding quotation. And speech is not as free as popularly imagined.

Because the U.S. Constitution says so little about speech, and many other things for that matter, what's "constitutional" is rarely a matter of what the Constitution actually says. Instead, it's what courts have, over the years, determined that it means—or what they have interpreted it to mean. Although the First Amendment is fairly absolute in its language, the reality is that the courts have decided that Congress can, in fact, abridge some categories of speech. In one key 2012 case, *United States v. Alvarez*, the U.S. Supreme Court laid out those categories to include:

1. advocacy intended, and likely, to incite imminent lawless action
2. obscenity
3. defamation
4. speech integral to criminal conduct
5. fighting words
6. child pornography
7. fraud
8. true threats
9. speech presenting some grave and imminent threat the government has the power to prevent[2]

That's a lot of categories, especially given the absolute language in the First Amendment itself, but courts have sought to strike a balance when one right or interest seriously conflicts with another. For example, if you threaten to kill someone, should your right to speech outweigh that person's right to life and safety? The courts have said no, and we're not arguing with them.

First Amendment law is highly complex and that's for a few reasons. First, the courts have determined, consistently and forcefully, that "speech" applies to a wide range of human expression—books, plays, posters, and comic books, for example, are all fair game. Music is definitely considered a form of expression that is protected by the First Amendment.

Just as important, especially for rap music, is that speech in all its forms is protected even if it's considered offensive or profane. (As a result, even so-called hate speech is actually protected by the First Amendment.) The Court has gone so far as to say, "The fact that society may find speech offensive is not a sufficient reason for suppressing it. Indeed, if it is the speaker's opinion that gives offense, that consequence is a reason for according it constitutional protection."[3]

For example, in one famous case, a Vietnam War protester named Paul Cohen was arrested for wearing a jacket with the words "FUCK THE DRAFT" emblazoned on it. The case made it all the way to the Supreme Court in 1971, which ultimately upheld Cohen's right to wear the jacket. Justice John Marshall Harlan, writing for the majority, homed in on the word "fuck" and noted that "one man's vulgarity is another's lyric." He went on to make a rather astute observation about art and expression:

> Much linguistic expression serves a dual communicative function: it conveys not only ideas capable of relatively precise, detached explication, but otherwise inexpress-

ible emotions as well. In fact, words are often chosen as much for their emotive as their cognitive force. We cannot sanction the view that the Constitution, while solicitous of the cognitive content of individual speech, has little or no regard for that emotive function which, practically speaking, may often be the more important element of the overall message sought to be communicated.

A much more recent case that illustrates how "offensive" rhetoric can serve multiple functions involves Simon Tam, the Asian American founder of a dance-rock band called The Slants.[4] When Tam attempted to register the name The Slants for a trademark, he was rejected by the Patent and Trademark Office because "slant"—a disparaging term for people of Asian descent—was considered offensive. The Supreme Court ruled that Tam was within his First Amendment rights to register the name.

For Tam, the goal was not to traffic in slurs but actually to reclaim the word and "drain its denigrating force."[5] For the Court, the decision was based on a fundamental fact: "Speech may not be banned on the ground that it expresses ideas that offend."

The Court has taken this position even when speech crosses the line from offensive to repugnant. In one case, anti-gay protesters from Westboro Baptist Church were picketing military funerals in order to draw attention to what they considered a growing, and immoral, tolerance of homosexuality in the United States. As part of their protest, some people yelled homophobic slurs or held signs that had distasteful slogans like "Fag troops" or "Thank God for dead soldiers." All this in front of grieving families.

Even though they protested in the most insensitive and offensive ways, they were doing so on public property, and the Supreme Court found that their speech was therefore protected by the First Amendment. In fact, the Court said that because the protesters were commenting on public issues, their speech was entitled to "special protection" under the First Amendment. Such speech, the Court argued, citing previous opinions, serves "the principle that debate on public issues should be uninhibited, robust, and wide-open" and therefore occupies the "highest rung of the hierarchy of First Amendment values."

The *public* aspect is especially important with respect to rap. Even when rappers seem to reject politics altogether or use lyrics that relish exaggerated stereotypes of black criminality, they are still engaging in a decidedly *public* critique. As scholar Imani Perry argues, the "in-your-face examples of black masculinity and excess that frighten the mainstream" are working to challenge the economic disenfranchisement black communities face. The use of such rhetoric, says Perry, "has been a long-standing strategy in black cultural politics."

Offensive expression that touches on public issues is not only protected by the First Amendment; it is the *most* protected form of expression, making First Amendment law seem perfectly tailored to rap music. Offensive to many? Check. Addresses public issues? Check.

And this takes us back to Jamal Knox and Rashee Beasley. There's little question that their song was a form of protest from two young men who had grown up feeling like they were unfairly targeted by their government.

Growing up, Knox had negative views on the criminal justice system broadly and police in particular. He recalls being "hassled" by officers even before entering middle school, developing a deep resentment. But he found some relief in poetry. Knox discovered the work of artists such as Maya Angelou, Langston Hughes, and Tupac Shakur. He wrote on his own in private. Then in middle school he met Leon Ford, the young man who was later shot and paralyzed by Pittsburgh police. In turn, Ford introduced Knox, who by then considered himself a poet, to the music recording studio.[6] Music became an outlet for him. Over the years, Knox's portfolio included a range of topics including mothering and God. He also wrote lyrics that were critical of violence.

Then, just seven months apart in 2012, Knox, Beasley, and Ford all had interactions with local police. In April, officers pulled over the vehicle driven by Jamal Knox. Beasley was a passenger in the car. During questioning, Knox sped off. He crashed the car and both men ran from the scene. Police caught up with them and arrested them. A search of Knox turned up fifteen small baggies of heroin and cash. During the search of his car police found a loaded, stolen firearm on the driver's side floorboard. Knox gave the arresting officer a false name. Later, another officer who arrived on the scene said he was familiar with Knox and Beasley and provided their true names. Knox and Beasley were charged with multiple offenses.[7] Then in November, Ford was shot.

That's when Knox and Beasley's version of "Fuck tha Police" was posted online. Years later (though it didn't come out at his trial), Knox remarked that the song was "a statement."[8] He intended it as protest.

There was plenty to protest, not just from their own experiences. In many black communities, often labeled "high-crime areas" by policymakers, there are clear tensions between residents and the police who monitor their communities. Their neighborhood in Pittsburgh was no different. As in many other black communities nationwide, some Pittsburgh residents' daily lives include encounters with police violence and brutality, including police shootings.[9] In 2010, eighteen-year-old Jordan Miles was beaten by three officers after they confronted him in the street on suspicion he possessed a weapon, and he resisted. In the end there was no gun. The case finally settled in 2016 for $125,000. Then in 2018, unarmed seventeen-year-old Antwon Jones was shot and killed by a police offer. That officer has since been criminally charged.[10] There are dozens more examples like this.

It's accepted knowledge that rap is sometimes used to comment on, and criticize, police misconduct and that it can be a vehicle for social and political protest, driven in large part by the realities of urban life for young black and Latino men.

That's why Knox's attorney argued that his song was protected by the First Amendment, and when the trial court disagreed, he appealed to the Pennsylvania Superior Court, the first level of review. The Superior Court declined to hear their case, but afterward the state Supreme Court agreed to hear it. At issue: "whether the First Amendment to the United States Constitution permits the imposition of criminal liability based on the publication of a rap-music video containing threatening lyrics directed to named law enforcement officers."[11]

In August 2018, that court concluded that the song was a true threat and not protected by the First Amendment. Its reasoning offers a glimpse at why courts have generally determined that rap isn't entitled to constitutional protection.

As it began to lay out its argument, the court opened with: "In many instances, lyrics along such lines cannot reasonably be understood as a sincere expression of the singer's intent to engage in real-world violence." So far so good. But the tenor quickly changed. The court went on to distinguish the song by Knox and Beasley, labeling it "of a different nature and quality." It concluded that the song did not "demonstrate an adherence to the distinction between singer and stage persona." In the court's estimation, the use of stage names, "fanciful" references, and "sophisticated production effects" was overshadowed by the specific "calling out" of the officers by name and "the clear expression repeated in various ways" that the officers were being "selectively targeted." The court concluded that the specificity "conflict[ed] with the contention that the song was meant to be understood as fiction."

In closing, the court remarked more broadly that

> if this Court were to rule that Appellant's decision to
> use a stage persona and couch his threatening speech as
> "gangsta rap" categorically prevented the song from being

construed as an expression of a genuine intent to inflict
harm, we would in effect be interpreting the Constitution
to provide blanket protection for threats, however severe,
so long as they are expressed within that musical style.

We've encountered this argument before. During oral arguments in
Elonis v. U.S., the threats case that went all the way to the U.S. Supreme
Court, Justice Samuel Alito claimed that providing First Amendment
protections for rap music would allow people to make threats and get
away with it if they did it in verse:

Well, this sounds like a roadmap for threatening a spouse
and getting away with it. So you—you put it in rhyme and
you put some stuff about the Internet on it and you say, I'm
an aspiring rap artist.
And so then you are free from prosecution.[12]

For Justice Alito and for the Pennsylvania Supreme Court, the
concern was that if they extended protections to rap music, they
would effectively be weakening their ability to punish threats. So
they made the argument we've seen in other threats cases as well:
that naming someone explicitly in a threatening lyric voids the lyric's
status as art.

We see this as bordering on the absurd. The legal standard that
seems to be developing is that in order to receive First Amendment
protection, rappers must speak in abstractions and generalities. But in
the context of rap, and other forms of expression, this standard makes
little sense. Rappers use real names or nicknames, theirs and others,
all the time in their songs. The inclusion of a real name doesn't necessarily diminish the artistic value. And the emphasis on name specificity makes less sense when one considers the particular category of
battle or diss raps. These raps often include real names because the
point is to focus on a particular person or thing.

So it is too simplistic for courts to presume that by naming a real person or thing the author is disseminating a true threat rather than throwing out a diss or engaging in the type of exaggerated, metaphorical, or fantastical verse that is typical of the genre. Something beyond the lyrics themselves should be offered to prove the unlawful threat. Otherwise, every battle or diss rap is unquestionably going to be declared unlawful, whether because it is a threat, defamatory, incitement, or fighting words. That outcome seems far too broad. After all, effigies of political figures—whether at Halloween or during political or social protests—are not subjected to such expansive proscription.[13] And how will we handle Facebook and Twitter battles?

Which leads us to the next problem we see. In some threats cases, in order to get around the obvious problem of punishing a work of art, judges have declared that either there is no pretense of entertainment by the defendant-artist or that by including threatening language, any such efforts have been abandoned, making the lyrics at issue unlawful threats. This was the rationale of the court in the *Knox* and *Beasley* cases. And this perspective was embraced by the government in the *Elonis* oral argument before the U.S. Supreme Court. During argument, Chief Justice John Roberts asked the deputy solicitor general, who was arguing on behalf of the federal government:

> If you have . . . a statement made in the style of rap music as this one or several of these were, is the reasonable person supposed to be someone familiar with that style and the use of what might be viewed as threatening words in connection with that music or is—or not [*sic*]?

The response was that context matters. If the speaker—that is, the rapper—is speaking to a general audience for the purpose of entertainment, that is understood differently than is speaking in private to an individual.

Later, Chief Justice Roberts quoted lyrics from Eminem's 1997 song "'97 Bonnie and Clyde":

> You know, "Da-da make a nice bed for mommy at the bottom of the lake," "tie a rope around a rock," this is during the context of a domestic dispute between a husband and wife. "There goes mama splashing in the water, no more fighting with dad."

The chief justice then asked the deputy solicitor general: "Under your test, could that be prosecuted [as a threat]?" The deputy solicitor general responded in the negative, stating, "Because Eminem said it at a concert where people are going to be entertained. This is a critical part of the context." He went on to say that in context, "any reasonable person would conclude at a minimum that there is ambiguity about these statements as being a serious intention of an expression to do harm. And this is critical here. We're talking about an area in which if the jury finds that it's ambiguous, it has to acquit. It has to conclude that this is how these statements should be interpreted."

So we see that context made all the difference in whether Eminem's lyrics had evidentiary value. According to the government's attorney, they didn't because the song was performed by a world-famous rapper at a concert of fans looking to be entertained.

That makes little sense. Eminem and others of his elite level shouldn't get a pass if no one else does. Those lyrics are not solely rapped by Eminem at large concerts. They are played over the airwaves, streamed over the Internet, and played in public spaces. Anyone (including Eminem's ex-wife and former romantic partners) can read or listen to him at virtually any time, in print and in digital form. Other artists, or just his fans, can listen to and recite his songs in their cars, in their bedrooms, at parties, and while they are walking down the street. It seems Eminem gets protection only when he performs at a large, public concert. What if he played or performed the song in private for a potential romantic partner? What if his ex-wife found the lyrics threatening, or, alternatively, she did not find them threatening but someone else thought they were threatening? Finally, imagine if no one found them threatening except the police and prosecutor.

There is no logic that justifies why a famous rapper should get more protection than an ordinary, amateur rapper in a courtroom. While many artists may not share the world stage with Eminem, the ever-present Internet makes for a huge platform. Fame is not easily defined; different people will reach different conclusions on whether someone is famous. How famous does the rapper have to be? Eminem is regarded as one of the genre's best lyricists. Should an undiscovered or recently discovered genius get the same treatment as Eminem? Justice Roberts seemed to be looking for answers to these questions. He didn't get any, and the Court didn't need to resolve them to make its decision. Sad to say, we have yet to see any court seriously grapple with them.[14]

In the vast majority of other cases where the lyrics themselves aren't being punished as threats, courts have found a way to exclude rap from First Amendment protections there, too. In cases where rap is used to demonstrate someone's guilt in an underlying crime, the government isn't directly acting to prohibit or punish art or expression. In other words, the government isn't creating a blanket rule that says citizens cannot create rap songs or that they face punishment if they do. While rap lyrics are being used to prove criminal cases, the lyrics themselves are not being punished directly. Instead, in most cases the lyrics are used to prove some past allegedly criminal activity. Essentially, then, courts are claiming that they aren't punishing speech; they are simply allowing it as evidence to prove a person's guilt for a crime they *can* punish.

Which brings us to a related aspect of this First Amendment claim: How do the rules of evidence operate in light of the First Amendment?

Which takes precedence? On this, the law is clear. The rules of evidence must give way to constitutional requirements for fair trials. But as the Pennsylvania court remarked when ruling on Knox's appeal, there is no legal basis under the evidence rules to discard otherwise admissible evidence:

> Appellant has appeared to labor under the belief that a person's speech is inadmissible at trial if it is constitutionally protected expression. There is no rule of evidence in Pennsylvania to that effect.

And there is no similar rule elsewhere. That's because courts haven't interpreted the First Amendment to apply to rules of evidence and legislatures haven't enacted rules prioritizing free speech over evidence. Each case, then, becomes a case-by-case assessment as to whether the rules of evidence permit or prohibit the evidence. And as we've seen, that's a train wreck.

What about chilling speech? Courts have agreed speech in its various forms needs to be protected against chilling effects—essentially, when the government's actions deter people from engaging in a protected activity.[15] We believe the potential for chilling effects is obvious. If a rap lyric can land you in jail, it follows that you'll think twice before writing one.

Recall the case of Olutosin Oduwole, the young man from Illinois who was convicted of making terroristic threats. In an interview shortly after he was released from prison, he said, "I still continue to make music. But now I'm a bit more aware of what I'm writing and making sure everything stays away from violence."[16] His speech got chilled.

Nevertheless, when defense attorneys have dared to suggest the First Amendment prohibits the use of rap as evidence because it punishes or chills free speech, courts have been dismissive. Given the scope of rap on trial and the massive potential for chilling effects, courts have an obligation to seriously reconsider their position.[17]

So what we're seeing is a systematic exclusion of rap music from the protection of the First Amendment. No matter that the music provides public commentary. No matter that punishing it, even indirectly, will undoubtedly chill it. No matter that courts are not applying their same faulty logic to other art forms.

Within the criminal legal process, it has become apparent that rapper defendants are not considered legitimate artists and rap music does not merit the artistic recognition granted to other forms of art. This perspective helps courts justify weaker First Amendment protections.[18]

Rap is not the only art to trade in outlaw, outlandish, and stereotypical narratives. It is not the only art form to draw from real life for its creations. It is not the only form of expression sometimes used as a tool of social protest. Yet is the only form of artistic expression to be mischaracterized as pure autobiography, real-world documentary.

Yes, the rules of evidence allow, in theory, for other musical genres and other art such as poetry, films, and novels to be used as evidence. But that rarely happens, and not in the same manner and to the same extent as with rap music. If the rules are being set aside or ignored for one type of art, that form is, for all intents and purposes, being restricted. That should implicate the First Amendment, no question, but it hasn't.

We have certainly looked for other examples of fiction being reclassified as autobiography and used to establish guilt in criminal cases. We haven't found much, even though plenty of other genres deal with violence and criminality that would, in theory, make them susceptible to similar punishments. Country music, with its long tradition of murder ballads? No. Heavy metal? Heavy metal has found itself in court, but usually in very different contexts. So no.

One somewhat tricky exception has been narcocorridos, which are songs specifically focused on drug trafficking and related offenses. They originate from northern Mexico and describe (or display, in the case of videos) real crime by Mexican drug cartels and members. Narcocorridos reside in a tradition of songs (corridos) that are distinctly *nonfiction*; they are often journalistic recounts of actual activities of drug traffickers, even though they are narrative in form, musical, and intended to entertain.[19] Many are commissioned by drug traffickers who want their exploits to be glorified in song.

The similarities between narcocorridos and gangsta rap have invited comparisons between the two. After all, they share common themes (i.e., criminal activities); both celebrate larger-than-life figures who operate beyond the control of an oppressive government; and both use slang and other poetic devices. There is, however, a meaningful difference between narcocorridos and rap. Rap is best understood as fictional, whereas the line between fiction and nonfiction in narcocorridos has become less clear as the genre has evolved away from straight nonfiction.

It turns out that police and prosecutors have used narcocorridos to investigate and prove their cases. As with rap, criminal investigators track online narcocorrido songs and videos.

In several cases we examined, prosecutors used the songs to paint stories of guilt or prove particular criminal activities. The government has also referenced them in support of sentencing recommendations.

Most interesting, prosecutors have justified the admission of narcocorridos by reference to the case law on rap music as criminal evidence. In a 2015 case, a federal prosecutor explicitly likened narcocorridos to "gangster rap" and cited cases involving the admission of rap music to advance the argument that the video and audio recordings and lyrics of a narcocorrido depicting the defendant's alleged gang activities were admissible. So here it's worth noting that while narcocorridos are a distinct genre, their use appears to be facilitated in part by prosecutors' use of rap.

Beyond music, we continue to look for cases in which evidence of other defendant-created art—particularly in the performing arts, literary arts, and visual arts—has similarly been used to prove guilt. While we have found criminal cases in which it would seem plausible that there might be artistic evidence applying the same logic courts have for rap, for the most part we find that either prosecutors haven't gone down that road or courts have ruled against admission.

State v. Hanson is most directly applicable.[20] In this Washington state decision from 1987, the appellate court held that the trial court erred in admitting evidence that the defendant had written crime fiction stories containing violence. A jury had convicted Hanson of assault. More specifically, the jury found him guilty of shooting a store clerk in the stomach. In his defense, he testified that he had "never committed a crime" and "never killed anyone." On cross examination, the prosecutor asked him about his hobby, fiction writing, and whether it contained violence. His defense attorney objected to the line of questioning. The court overruled the objection. Hanson then admitted that he had written about violence involving Vietnam veterans (he had served in Vietnam) and a remarried widower who becomes violent toward his wife when she "turns on him" (he was a remarried widower who was planning to divorce at the time of the alleged crime).

Hanson appealed his conviction. He lodged several claims, including that the evidence of his fictional writings was improperly admitted. The court held that the writings were not indicative of whether Hanson had a violent character, stating: "A writer of crime fiction . . . can hardly be said to have displayed criminal propensities through works he or she has authored." The court further explained: "The crime charged was a random, brutal act of violence for which there was no apparent motive. By suggesting that the defendant's character conformed to the violent acts in his writings, the State supplied the jury with an improper explanation for why the defendant would have committed the crime charged." On this basis, the court reversed and remanded for a new trial. At his second trial, the jury acquitted, but by this time he had already been incarcerated for eighteen months.[21]

More than thirty years have passed since *Hanson* was decided. Over that period, few courts have seriously grappled with the applicability of that decision when the writings were fictional rap lyrics, not crime fiction. Of those that have, they have distinguished *Hanson* or decided it doesn't apply, concluding that while fictional writing may not be used to prove character, it may be relevant to prove intent or knowledge.[22] Based on this reasoning, those courts have tended to deem lyrics admissible, finding the lyrics were permissible evidence of mental state for the crime charged.[23] Two exceptions are the Court of Appeals of Maryland in *Hannah v. State* and the New Jersey Supreme Court in *State v. Skinner*, both of which ruled in favor of the defendants based on the facts of those cases.[24]

Freedom of Speech . . . Just Watch What You Say!

We are simply not finding widespread examples in which fictional genres are being read by courts as true-to-life representations of the author's thoughts or actions.[25] That's because prosecutors haven't tried it yet or because when they do, courts shut them down, as in *Hanson*. The other reason is that the First Amendment doesn't seem to be operating here. When rap lyrics are deemed inadmissible, courts cite the rules of evidence, not the First Amendment, just as they did in *Hanson*.

Because of this, we think the First Amendment law actually leaves rap open to additional vulnerabilities. In fact, some of the earliest legal attacks on rap music were rooted in First Amendment law. At the top of this chapter, we listed various categories of speech that are not protected by the First Amendment. One of them is obscenity. According to the Supreme Court, something is obscene if (1) it appeals to the prurient interest, meaning a morbid, unusual, or unhealthy interest in nudity, sex, obscenity, or pornography, (2) it depicts, in a patently offensive way, sexual conduct defined by state law, and (3) it lacks serious literary, artistic, political, or scientific value.[26]

In the late 1980s and early 1990s, as rap began to explode in popularity, authorities across the country used obscenity laws in order to silence artists whose lyrics or performances they found objectionable. For Luther Campbell and his rap group 2 Live Crew, that meant having an entire album declared illegal due to a federal judge's ban of the sale of *As Nasty as They Wanna Be* across much of southern Florida. The judge ruled that the 1989 album, with tracks like "Me So Horny" and "Dick Almighty," was legally obscene. "It is an appeal to dirty thoughts and the loins, not to the intellect and the mind," Judge Jose Gonzales wrote in his opinion.[27]

The judge's ruling gave police the authority that they sought, and they soon arrested a record store owner who refused to stop selling the album. They also arrested all of the members of the group and eventually took them to trial for violating obscenity laws.

At the highly publicized, closely watched trial, the defense called music critic John Leland and renowned literary critic Henry Louis Gates Jr. to attest to the artistic merits of the music and the importance of understanding black vernacular traditions.[28] Among other things, Gates argued that the exaggeration in the lyrics served a political goal, which was to blow up popular stereotypes about black sexuality by presenting those stereotypes in an extreme and comical form.

In the end, the jury sided with Gates and 2 Live Crew by finding the group not guilty of violating obscenity laws. Two years later, in 1992, the Eleventh Circuit U.S. Court of Appeals overturned Gonzales's original decision, noting that he had not shown that *As Nasty as They Wanna Be* lacked artistic merit. After the jury trial acquittal and then the Eleventh Circuit decision, Luther Campbell proclaimed victory. "What this does is let black folks know that the First Amendment really does apply to us," he said. "It says we can speak our minds the same way that white people do."[29]

We're not so sure it does. Yes, courts were poised to protect rap from a frontal assault on obscenity grounds, an approach that, as many people at the time noted, could have implications for white artists as well. But it didn't follow that courts had accepted the arguments of Gates and others that rap music was a legitimate art form worthy of broad First Amendment protections. It just meant that if law enforcement wanted to put rap music and the people behind it on trial, they'd have to find another way.

And in the years since, they have. As we've seen, authorities began to silence rap via the threats exception, rather than obscenity. And given the long-standing antipathy toward rap within the criminal justice system, as well as courts' reluctance to view rap as protected speech, we find it possible, even likely, that rappers will eventually be fending off legal attacks when their lyrics are deemed defamatory, as incitements to violence, or as fighting words—all categories of speech that courts have said do not enjoy First Amendment protections.

We are in a pivotal moment with respect to the First Amendment and rap music. In recent years the Supreme Court has passed on the opportunity to articulate its view on the extent to which rap is protected speech (in *Elonis*, the court avoided the broader First Amendment issues). Jamal Knox wanted to give them another shot. After he lost his appeal to the Pennsylvania Supreme Court, he decided to take his case to the U.S. Supreme Court. Despite support for his appeal from well-known rappers such as Killer Mike, Chance the Rapper, and Meek Mill (and even Luther Campbell), the Court ultimately declined to hear his case.

Although the Supreme Court won't have a chance to address it, the *Knox* case presents for us another significant concern. At Knox's and Beasley's trial, the only witnesses to offer any information or opinion on the song were law enforcement witnesses. One explained how he came across the song. He then interpreted some of the words and phrases, based on the time he spent "interacting with individuals in the relevant neighborhood" and learning "some of their street slang."[30] He also listened to another song by Knox and Beasley and based his interpretation on those earlier lyrics. The others named in the song testified how they personally reacted to the lyrics.

But we question the officers' qualifications to interpret the song in the first place.

5

Aggressive Prosecutors and Untrained Experts

For Deandre Mitchell, November 13, 2014, was bittersweet. After spending two years in jail, awaiting trial for his alleged role in a 2012 shooting in Antioch, California, he decided to accept a plea bargain for a lesser charge, and with that, he was a free man.[1]

Mitchell's case dates back to September 2012, when, according to witnesses, two men fired approximately ten rounds at a forty-five-year-old man in an apparent drive-by shooting. One of the bullets hit the man in the chest, narrowly missing his vital organs; he survived.

Police suspected that the shooting was a gang-related retaliation by members of the Deep C, or Deep Central gang, based in nearby Richmond, California. Mitchell was one of the suspects, and after being indicted for attempted murder in October 2012, he was arrested and detained in jail. With bail set at an astronomical $6 million, he—like countless Americans across the country—had no choice but to spend years behind bars waiting for his trial.

His release was bittersweet because the father of two had already given up two years of his life to the criminal justice system, all for a crime he maintains he never committed. He ultimately pled guilty, not because prosecutors had a strong case against him but, ironically, because they didn't. There was no physical evidence connecting him to the crime, and it turns out that the victim, who had originally claimed he saw Mitchell at the shooting, actually admitted to police that he'd heard a *rumor* that Mitchell was involved; he didn't actually see him.[2]

With such a weak case, the prosecutor, a deputy district attorney for Contra Costa County named Satish Jallepalli, looked for other evidence. He found it in the form of rap videos that Mitchell—also known as Laz tha Boy, an aspiring rapper with a growing Bay Area fan base—had posted to YouTube. Even though Mitchell's videos had been made years earlier and didn't include any references to the shootings he was charged with, Jallepalli argued to a grand jury that the videos illustrated Mitchell's mind-set, his willingness to commit the crimes, and his willingness to commit them on behalf of Deep C.

It's worth pausing for a moment to point out the important difference between a grand jury proceeding and an actual trial. The purpose of a grand jury is to determine whether there is probable cause to believe (1) that a crime has been committed and (2) that the accused person committed it. In theory, a grand jury acts as a filter of sorts, screening out cases that lack sufficient evidence to warrant a trial. Because the grand jury isn't determining guilt, the rules of a trial don't apply. The proceedings happen in secret and are rarely made available to the public afterward. The accused is generally not involved at all, and neither is a defense attorney. There is no judge present to provide oversight or make rulings.

This is the prosecutor's show—he or she chooses which witnesses to call (and often will only present a law enforcement officer), conducts all questioning, and instructs the grand jury on the rules of law. In order to indict, grand juries do not have to reach a unanimous decision, and if the grand jury declines to indict, the prosecutor can simply present the case a second time to the same grand jury or to a different one. Because the process is so one-sided, it's often said by prosecutors and defense attorneys alike that you could indict a ham sandwich.

With the rules stacked in his favor, Jallepalli was able to depict

Mitchell's lyrics and videos without any regard for them as artistic creations. In front of the grand jury, he referred to the rap videos—some of which had amassed several hundred thousand views—as "gang videos." The experts he called to offer their analysis of rap lyrics were actually Richmond gang detectives with no special knowledge of the Bay Area music scene or rap music.

When Jallepalli asked one detective, John Lopez, to explain the meaning of various phrases from Mitchell's videos, Lopez offered implausible interpretations. He claimed, for instance, that "to 'ride' is to shoot . . . If you're a rider, you're a shooter."[3]

That's nonsense. "To ride," taken literally, is to go for a ride, as in a car. Figuratively, especially in rap music, it means to be loyal or devoted. Not even in the depths of Urban Dictionary, an online crowd-sourced dictionary of slang terms and phrases, can you find a definition that says a rider is a shooter. And when asked to explain "Do it for the block" (a phrase repeated in the song "What U Do It Fo")— he responded, "Doing it for your—in essence, Deep C, whether it be crimes and/or shootings." Aside from the fact that "crimes and/or shootings" suggests that shootings aren't crimes, the problem is that Lopez takes a generic refrain like "Do it for the block"—used verbatim in songs by well-known artists—and offers a highly detailed interpretation that just happens to fit the prosecutor's argument to a T. Even though Mitchell doesn't say that he commits crimes for Deep C or any other gang, a police detective with no expertise in rap music sat before a grand jury and said he did.

With the rules stacked in his favor, Jallepalli was able to depict Mitchell's lyrics and videos without any regard for them as artistic creations. The grand jury indicted Mitchell on all counts.

Mitchell maintained his innocence, but even with no good evidence against him, he and his attorney, John Hamasaki, understood that if he went to trial, prosecutors would likely try to introduce those same videos, along with the same "expert" testimony from gang detectives. With a potentially conservative jury in Contra Costa County, Mitchell made what he would later describe as "the hardest decision of my life": he pleaded to a lesser charge, assault with a firearm, and avoided the much steeper sentence he would have faced if jurors decided to punish Deandre Mitchell for the words of Laz tha Boy.[4]

For decades police and prosecutors have prioritized gang prosecutions, deploying multiple tactics and significant resources to identify and break up alleged criminal street gangs. This effort has been facilitated by anti-gang laws, special gang prosecutors, and the use of so-called gang experts. Operating in unison, these measures have fueled the increasing use of rap lyrics as criminal evidence and provided judges and juries with inaccurate, unreliable interpretations of lyrics, with sometimes devastating results for defendants.

Mitchell's case is far from unique. Across the country, police and prosecutors routinely use rap videos in order to establish a defendant's connection to a gang. The reason is simple: in a number of states— as we saw earlier, California foremost among them—prosecutors can pursue a gang enhancement, which allows them to seek much steeper sentences if they can show that a crime was committed on behalf of, or in association with, a gang. Depending on the crime, an enhancement can result in a far longer prison term. For instance, in California, carjacking ordinarily carries a sentence of anywhere from three to nine years.[5] But if prosecutors can demonstrate that the carjacking was somehow gang related, they can demand fifteen years minimum.[6] And in a number of states, prosecutors are permitted to charge juveniles as adults if they can demonstrate that the alleged crime was gang related.[7] So enhancements are a big deal.

And prosecutors seek them all the time. It isn't particularly difficult. For starters, police departments across the country maintain secretive, often expansive, databases of so-called validated or verified gang members in their community. It doesn't take much to add people to the database. Generally, police rely on a checklist of gang-like characteristics, and if people meet just two or three items on that checklist, they can be added to the gang database.[8] In many jurisdictions, there's no meaningful way to challenge or appeal your inclusion on the list, and police are not required to inform you that you've been added.

In California, for example, police use the following checklist to determine whether they can add someone to CalGang, the notoriously large and poorly maintained statewide gang database. (It has roughly 150,000 people in it.) A person has to meet just two of the criteria, with the exception of item 10, which can be the sole criterion.

1. Subject has admitted to being a gang member.
2. Subject has been arrested with known gang members for offenses consistent with gang activity.
3. Subject has been identified as a gang member by a reliable informant/source.
4. Subject has been identified as a gang member by an untested informant.
5. Subject has been seen affiliating with documented gang members.
6. Subject has been seen displaying gang symbols and/or hand signs.
7. Subject has been seen frequenting gang areas.
8. Subject has been seen wearing gang dress.
9. Subject is known to have gang tattoos.
10. In-custody classification interview.

Many of these items rely on a significant amount of discretion from individual police officers or are so broad that they could apply to entire neighborhoods. If you live in a neighborhood in which gangs are active, for example, you could easily get a check for item 7. If you happen to talk to or conduct any legitimate business with any gang members in your neighborhood, even family members or classmates, you just checked item 5. And God forbid you wear a Dallas Cowboys jersey in Crip territory (Crips are associated with the color blue) or an Arizona Cardinals jersey in a Blood neighborhood (Bloods are associated with red). That just checked item 8. You're already at three strikes, more than enough to be eligible for CalGang. That means that anyone affiliating with *you* just got a strike, too.

With police as the sole arbiters of who is included and who isn't (although some communities have added more transparency), gang databases allow police to surveil and criminalize entire communities—almost always communities of color. Roughly 85 percent of people in CalGang are black or Latino. What's more, with no oversight, you get mistakes. Indeed, a recent audit of CalGang showed the database was teeming with inaccuracies. One of the most absurd: forty-two people listed were under one year old. According to the database, twenty-eight of them admitted to being a gang member—a stunning linguistic feat.[9]

Whether it's California or any other state that allows for gang enhancements, if you're designated as a gang member in a police database and are accused of a crime, it's very likely that prosecutors will seek a gang enhancement if they can. Even if a suspect's not in the gang database, prosecutors can still seek a gang enhancement. All they need is to offer evidence in court that the defendant associates with gang members; then they can argue that the crime he or she is charged with was done on behalf of those gang members.

A prosecutor training manual written in 2004 by a Los Angeles assistant district attorney for a national organization of prosecutors reveals the kinds of evidence that gang investigators are encouraged to look for to draw these connections. Notice the not-so-subtle assumption, evident in the physical description of the "real" defendant's do-rag, that the person on trial will be black:

> Perhaps the most crucial element of a successful prosecution is introducing the jury to the real defendant. Invariably, by the time the jury sees the defendant at trial, his hair has grown out to a normal length, his clothes are nicely tailored, and he will have taken on the aura of an altar boy. But the *real* defendant is a criminal wearing a do-rag and throwing a gang sign. Gang evidence can take a prosecutor a long way toward introducing the jury to that person. Through photographs, letters, notes, and even music lyrics, prosecutors can invade and exploit the defendant's true personality. Gang investigators should focus on these items of evidence during search warrants and arrests.[10]

To be clear, "music lyrics" means rap lyrics. Gang investigators aren't combing through notebooks and hard drives for country music.

And it may come as no surprise that police and prosecutors are drawn to lyrics that can be loosely categorized within the broad field of gangsta rap, a label that today serious fans of rap and the music industry would find unhelpful. That's because the label itself offers a competitive advantage in the courtroom, just as it did in commercial sales. It allows prosecutors to imbue their courtroom narrative with the specter of gang violence. Additionally, it evokes images of hypermasculinity, criminality, and the thuggishness that the public, hence jurors, may accept as accurate depictions of the black or Latino male defendants in these cases. In this way, prosecutors profit from uncritically deploying the gangsta rap label.

Of course, police and prosecutors didn't just stick to the script and look for music lyrics.

Enter rap videos. If you ever watch rap videos online, particularly from aspiring rappers, you immediately notice some similarities among them. Lyrically and visually, they often emphasize features of the local environment—street signs, local businesses, or particular blocks unique to that community. One of the predominant images in these videos is the intersection—many videos offer close-ups or still shots of the street signs that sit at the intersection of two roads. They also feature lots of people, often residents of the neighborhood, who serve as extras, so to speak. The video may feature one or more rappers, but just behind them is often a crowd of people bobbing to the beat or singing along to the lyrics. It's a way for aspiring rappers to suggest their popularity—wherever they go, crowds follow—but also to represent their neighborhood and the people who live there.

It's also an easy way for police and prosecutors to get gang enhancements. In case after case, we have seen prosecutors use a single rap video to indict and pursue gang charges against multiple people who simply appeared in the background, even when they had no role in writing the lyrics or producing the video. It's flawed logic at best. If prosecutors can identify at least one person in the video who is a validated gang member, then they can argue that everyone else in the video is affiliated with the gang. It's guilt by association.

In fact, it turns out that Satish Jallepalli, the prosecutor in Deandre Mitchell's case, takes this approach himself. Not only did Jallepalli use Mitchell's videos to indict him and extract a plea bargain, but it turns out he also used one of his videos in a separate case against a Richmond, California, man named Desean Haywood, who was charged with a 2011 home invasion robbery.[11] During the grand jury proceeding for Haywood, Jallepalli introduced "Southside Richmond," another song by Laz tha Boy (and featuring two other rappers, Tay-Way and Young-Bo). He played the video for the song and provided jurors with a copy of the song's lyrics, which he had transcribed himself. When he reached the line "*Erv*, like you in the game, and you niggas running backs," he asked police gang detective Matt Anderson to explain.

Anderson testified, without hesitation, that the line referred to Ervin Coley, a rival gang member murdered in 2011. Except he was way off. Young-Bo's line is "*Urlacher* in the game, man you niggas running back," which he punctuates in the video by pretending to run backward.[12] "Urlacher," of course, refers to Hall of Fame professional football player Brian Urlacher, one of the most famous linebackers to play the game. Jallepalli and Anderson totally fabricated the gang connection in that lyric, which Anderson essentially admitted under cross examination when he said, "I don't know if that was actually said in the song."

(In at least one other case, Jallepalli has admitted that he was actually corrected by a juror when his expert attributed a number of violent lyrics to a defendant. In a note, the juror pointed out the lyrics were written by well-known rap artists, not the defendant.)

At Haywood's trial, Jallepalli continued his practice, introducing the video for Mitchell's "What U Do It Fo" (also used against Mitchell). It's a video that's consistent with that of many aspiring rappers. It opens with shots of a local housing complex, followed by a close-up of street signs at an intersection—in this case at 4th Street and McDonald Avenue in Richmond. For much of the rest of the video, we see Mitchell (as Laz tha Boy) alongside another rapper, Cool da Goon, in many scenes flanked by dozens of young men from the neighborhood.

Haywood is among them. He doesn't perform in the video and had nothing to do with its creation. He's just standing in the background. While some of the young men make gestures that look like guns or gang signs, Haywood doesn't. He just bobs his head to the beat. But that was good enough for Jallepalli. He introduced the video, in his words, "to prove [Haywood's] affiliation with a gang and his prior contact with a gang."[13]

Defense attorneys have shared with us stories of a single video being used to charge multiple people, many of them doing the same thing as Haywood. Even when the person is not a gang member, isn't doing anything to suggest gang affiliation, and had nothing to do with the creation of the song, prosecutors use the video to get a gang enhancement.

It's a cynical tactic. It allows prosecutors to threaten people who are obviously not gang members with a steep sentence if they don't accept a plea agreement. Haywood took the case to trial anyway and got lucky—the jury didn't buy the gang charge. But many others, like Mitchell, take the plea deal to avoid the risk. In fact, more than 90 percent of federal and state felony cases end in a guilty plea. Defendants plead guilty to receive lesser sentences, although many are still incarcerated for lengthy periods of time.

One, a Sacramento man named BillyDee Smith, was facing a charge for weapons possession. Prosecutors used his appearance in the background of videos produced by rappers Mozzy and Philthy Rich—both well-known and accomplished artists from the Sacramento area—to argue that the possession was gang related. But Smith was not a validated gang member. What's more, in at least one video, while everyone else is wearing black, white, and red clothing (which police claimed was gang attire even though much of it was obviously merchandise from Mozzy's label), Smith was wearing Florida Marlins gear. Orange and turquoise aren't identifiable gang colors for anybody in California.

Nevertheless, Smith decided to plead guilty to a lesser charge rather than face the videos at trial.

Questionable Gang "Expertise"

A 2008 article in *Police: The Law Enforcement Magazine* argues that prosecutors should look to establish gang connections in their cases because "gang allegations and enhancements can multiply criminal penalties substantially. They are highly prejudicial and do great damage to the defense."[14]

In many cases, that is of course the point. Police and prosecutors don't always know or care if someone is connected to a gang. They just know that if they make the allegation, however indefensible, they can smear a defendant's reputation in front of a judge and jury. To do this, prosecutors often rely on a so-called gang expert.

Generally speaking, expert witnesses are called to provide opinions on matters of fact relevant to the case at hand. Unlike lay witnesses, who are only permitted to testify based on what they have witnessed or observed, expert witnesses can go much further. Provided they have the specialized training, education, or experience to do so, they can offer opinions in front of a judge and jury about facts that are related to their area of expertise. And they do not have to base their opinions on their personal observations or experiences. The expert, therefore, can be vital to the outcome of a trial.

The problem, however, is that although the term "expert" implies a substantial level of actual training, education, knowledge, or credentials, the legal standard is surprisingly flexible for who can be deemed an expert in a particular subject. In judicial settings, experts usually don't need to have any specific set of qualifications (with some exceptions). Evidence rules uniformly give judges the authority to prevent insufficiently knowledgeable witnesses from serving as experts and exclude unreliable expert testimony. However, the legal system doesn't place excessive value on the kinds of credentials most of us would assume a so-called expert to have, such as graduate school training, formal research experience, and industry-recognized certifications. Experts may have those high-level credentials or may be qualified based simply on professional experience, training, and practice. The low level of required qualifications led one legal commenter to ask, "Should we expect the judicial branch of our government to employ a standard of 'expertise' at least as rigorous as the one used by, say, *Dateline NBC*?"[15]

Unfortunately, the judiciary doesn't, and that becomes immediately apparent when it comes to gang experts. The authors of one study found that gang experts are not, in fact, experts on much at all:

> The gang unit officers whom we studied were, for the most part, poorly trained on gang-related matters. Although all officers received mandated broad police training, most gang units did not require training specific to their officers' positions, at least not beyond basic elements such as documenting gang members, using the gang information system, and an introduction to gang culture. As a consequence, officers were primarily trained by their on-the-job experiences. This method was found to result in several problems affecting their criminal investigations, dissemination of intelligence, and capacity to provide reliable information to policymakers and community members.[16]

Many police officers lack formal education beyond a high school degree. They tend, in many cases, to work with local gangs as part of their official function. They rarely conduct or publish in-depth studies or formal research, either local, regional, or national in scope. They do not always learn from impartial, neutral teachers or training programs. Aside from what they learned at the police academy, the extent of their expertise derives from their on-the-job observations, supplemented with the occasional training seminar that might last anywhere from an afternoon to several days. Those seminars aren't necessarily the most rigorous. Some may be conducted by other government-employed police officers or prosecutors, who may also be lacking in qualifications. And some receive their training from commercial organizations such as The Gang Enforcement Company, LLC, for instance, which offers a "Basic Gangology Specialist Certification" via its Florida-based training center. It's just $197—probably because it's marketed as an online self-study course that can be completed "from the comfort of your home or office." There are also budget options; for just $30, officers can receive focused training on graffiti or hate groups, sent right to their email accounts, which can be completed in as little as one hour.[17]

Needless to say, gang "expertise" is not necessarily hard to come by, and there is no central accrediting body recognized by courts to ensure that training is accurate or rigorous. Because of gang experts' lack of clear training or credentialing, one legal scholar has argued that their testimony should be excluded altogether.[18]

But it's usually permitted, and the result is that gang experts sometimes offer questionable testimony about gangs. When they, or prosecutors, start to opine about rap or hip hop—topics on which they have absolutely no training or experience—their testimony is often a disaster. It results in inaccurate, or flatly incorrect, representations of rap music and, by extension, the defendant. In most cases, defense attorneys don't have an expert on rap music to rebut the gang expert's testimony, so these representations go unchallenged. And some of the errors that police and prosecutors make are egregious.

For instance, *U.S. v. Gerald Johnson*: In 2015, Baltimore native and alleged gang member Gerald Johnson was tried in Baltimore circuit court for murder, robbery, and drug charges. He was acquitted on all counts.[19] In 2017, he was retried at the federal level, largely for the same allegations. At trial federal prosecutors, particularly motivated to secure a conviction after the state-level acquittal, introduced a number of rap lyrics performed by Johnson. They also introduced a photo they took from Johnson's phone, which they alleged was a recent photo of a key gang member related to the case. Not quite. It was a photo of rapper Notorious B.I.G. standing next to fellow rapper Craig Mack (authorities believed Mack was the key gang member). The photo, widely circulated online, had been taken decades earlier. Johnson had it on his phone because, like just about every aspiring rapper, he admired Notorious B.I.G. (who died in 1997). Anyone with even a passing knowledge of hip hop would recognize a picture of Notorious B.I.G. Johnson was found guilty and sentenced to life in prison without parole. At sentencing, the judge said Johnson posed "perhaps the greatest danger of any defendant the court has ever sentenced," a view that was very different from the Baltimore jury that had acquitted him.

There is also *State v. Christopher Bassett*: In 2017 Knoxville, Tennessee, prosecutors charged three young men with the murder of Zaevion Dobson. It was a high-profile case; President Barack Obama himself had talked publicly about Dobson, a high school student who was caught in the crossfire of a conflict between rival gang members. At trial, prosecutors introduced a rap video involving the three young men charged with the crime in order to establish their gang affiliations. The defense attorneys for one of the men, Christopher Bassett, called one of this book's authors (Erik) as an expert witness. On cross examination, the prosecutor—getting his information from a gang expert who earlier testified about rap and said, "It's not my favorite type of music"—began by asking if it was true that the top fifty rappers are all gang members. Shocked at the ridiculousness of the question, Erik replied that no, that was definitely not true. The prosecutor then thundered back, "What about Suge Knight!?" When Erik responded that Suge Knight wasn't a rapper but a music producer, he began to realize that he was working with some bad information. That was one of several major oversights or outright mistakes that prosecutors made in that trial with respect to rap music.

There was also *Commonwealth v. Maurice Patterson*: During the 2010 murder trial of Pennsylvania man Maurice Patterson—a trial in which prosecutors were seeking the death penalty—prosecutors introduced a handwritten letter dated March 25, 2007, in which Patterson included the sentence "When I gave [*sic*] the word tear that ass out the frame." Prosecutors asserted that the phrase "tear that ass out the frame"—which, according to Patterson, came from a song by rapper Tupac Shakur—was an instruction to carry out a murder. To support its argument, the Commonwealth argued that only one song by Tupac Shakur, "Homeboyz," ever contained the phrase "tear that ass out the frame." The lyrical context of that one song, particularly the line "Woke up on the street, but you'll be sleepin' in the casket," made it clear, they argued, that "tear that ass out the frame" was indeed a reference to murder.

Patterson insisted that he was talking about putting his drug-dealing competition out of business, not murder. He testified that he didn't recognize the lyrics to the song prosecutors were referring to. The jury was unmoved. Patterson was convicted and sentenced to death.

The problem is that the prosecutors were wrong. A version of Shakur's lyrics in "Homeboyz" (including the phrase "tear that ass out the frame") also appeared in a remix called "Bitch Please III," featuring Shakur himself alongside rappers Eminem, Xzibit, Snoop Dogg, Nate Dogg, Ja Rule, and DMX. Importantly, in the remixed version, the lyrics that prosecutors focused on to make their argument—especially the line "you'll be sleepin' in the casket"—are missing altogether. Because the lyric was an important part of the case and his conviction, Patterson is appealing from death row.

There was also *State v. Alex Medina:* In 2013, prosecutors in Ventura County, California, put eighteen-year-old Alex Medina on trial for murder, charging him as an adult for a crime he was accused of committing four years earlier. Rap lyrics that they found in Medina's notebooks—some of them written well before the crime, and some written in detention afterward—became a significant part of their case as they tried to establish a gang connection (to secure a gang enhancement). At trial, the District Attorney described rap lyrics as "autobiographical journals" and in its trial brief, submitted to the court to explain its theory of the case, the state includes page after page of rap lyrics, along with an attempt to provide analysis, much of it provided by their investigator and their gang expert, Detective Steven Jenkins.

Here's an example where prosecutors cite a lyric and then explain how it fits their theory of the case. Because the lyrics here were written after the crime, prosecutors want to characterize them as confessions:

> People's Exhibits 133–141 are gang writings found in the defendant's cell on October 11, 2009. In People's Exhibit 133, the defendant writes, "Put me down for murder in the first degree." This either references his willingness to murder for his gang or the fact that he has already done so; in either case, it is a highly incriminating statement. He also writes, "Everyone around me has killed b4," implying that he is now in an elite class of gang bangers who have committed murder.
>
> In People's Exhibit 134, the defendant refers to himself as a "baby veterano." In gang culture, a member achieves "veterano," or veteran, status only by putting in significant work for the gang, work being criminal activity. The fact that defendant would refer to himself in this manner implies he has put in significant work for the gang. Given his young age, it would appear he is referencing committing a particularly serious crime rather than committing less [sic] crimes over an extended period.

The specificity of the analysis, and all of the detail extracted from just one phrase, is somewhat odd, but it turns out to be a downright tragedy. Neither prosecutors, nor their investigator, nor their "expert" realized that these lyrics weren't Medina's at all. The lyrics in the first paragraph (above) are from word-for-word transcriptions of the song "Bloody War" by rap artist South Park Mexican, a favorite of Medina's.

It somehow eludes everyone that, at the very top of the page (on its own line), Medina writes "Bloody War—SPM."

And the claim that "baby veterano" signaled that Medina had just done something major and ominous for the gang was another mistake. That lyric was from a word-for-word transcription of a song called "The Danger Zone" by Chicano group Charlie Row Campo. The video has nearly a million hits on YouTube.[20]

These kinds of mistakes are common and predictable, but they are also unacceptable. Obviously if someone with no training related to rap music takes the stand as an expert and proceeds to offer expert testimony related to rap lyrics or videos, that testimony is going to be wildly unreliable. It's tempting to blame prosecutors and the law enforcement gang experts themselves. They know full well that testimony like this will only intensify the prejudicial impact of the music. Indeed, when gang experts go out of their way to tell juries that they dislike rap, just before they go on to offer expert testimony about it (yes, this happens), they are confirming that rap is so prejudicial that they feel the need to distance themselves from it in front of a jury.

In an adversarial system, it's hard to blame one side for doing everything it can within the rules to win. Most of the time we applaud criminal defense attorneys who do that. That's their official job: to zealously defend their clients. But it's different for prosecutors, so we can place some of the blame on them. Their job is to secure justice, not to win at all costs and not to be so blinded by the desire to convict someone, anyone, that they use unfair tactics or convict the innocent. But fine. Prosecutors and defense attorneys do what they can for their side. So then the problem is that judges—the gatekeepers of the process—are too often asleep at the wheel or, worse, complicit in the prosecutor's game. According to Supreme Court rulings and the federal rules of evidence, trial judges are supposed to closely scrutinize the qualifications of experts as well as the data, principles, and methods on which those experts base their opinions.[21] The judges' job is to keep out bad "experts" and bad "expertise." They are the backstop. Despite this mandate, however, all too often trial judges are not performing that function. One study from 2001 revealed that judges often do not understand the legal standard for expert testimony, and they may lack the appropriate knowledge to evaluate the quality of the evidence.[22]

There are important exceptions, however. Perhaps the most notable is found in the case of Lamory Gray, a Massachusetts man who was convicted of first-degree murder in part because of a rap video that prosecutors introduced at trial to establish his connection to a gang.[23] Gray was willing to stipulate to gang membership just so prosecutors wouldn't introduce the prejudicial video. As in many of the cases we've seen, Gray wasn't one of the artists being featured in the video—he was standing with a dozen other guys in the background, while the main performer delivered lines like "forty four by my side" or "we have pills, perps, pistols and powder. It's a P-Thang."

At trial, the video was identified and introduced by a Boston police sergeant who testified that all he knew of rap music was from what he heard when his kids were in the car. Later in the trial, prosecutors also referred to statements made by another police officer, a gang expert, who had characterized the video as evidence of gang membership. Again, Gray was willing to stipulate that he was in a gang just to avoid having the jury see the video.

After he was convicted, Gray appealed, and the case was ultimately heard by the Supreme Judicial Court of Massachusetts, the state's highest court. The justices reversed Gray's conviction, in large part because of the prejudicial impact of the video and their understanding that rap music shouldn't be interpreted literally. Unlike most courts across the country, the Massachusetts court recognized—and rejected—the artistic double standard underlying rap on trial. To quote the court: "We discern no reason why rap music lyrics, unlike any other musical form, should be singled out and viewed *sui generis* as literal statements of fact or intent."

Just as important, the court made it clear that gang experts, generally speaking, do not have the necessary expertise to interpret rap music: "A police officer who has been qualified as a 'gang expert' cannot, without more, be deemed an expert qualified to interpret the meaning of rap music lyrics."

There is no doubt that some officers in gang units across the country have specialized local knowledge that makes their testimony valuable in certain gang-related cases. But by allowing them to testify to the meaning or significance of a highly complex art form that they have little or no familiarity with, courts are refusing to acknowledge that rap music is an art form, or that its creators are artists, which in the process gives prosecutors yet another tool with which to incarcerate young men of color. The Massachusetts Supreme Court managed to grasp at least some of the problems with that, but nationwide that has been far from the case.

6

Surveillance, Suppression, and the Rise of Gang Units

May 10, 2007. Sixteen-year-old Christopher Horton and his friend Brian Dean, twenty, were sitting on the front porch of Horton's home in the South Precinct of Newport News, Virginia. Suddenly somebody approached the house and shot both of them, killing Horton immediately and sending Dean to the hospital with a gunshot wound to the head. He was taken off life support the following day.

Two people were gunned down in broad daylight, yet the ensuing police investigation turned up next to nothing: no witnesses, no murder weapon, no suspects. As a result, the case went cold for years until, in 2011, a new detective, Carlos Nunez, was assigned to the investigation. Like the detectives before him, Nunez faced the daunting task of solving a crime that was several years old and that, at the time, left few clues to the identity of the killer. But eventually a new lead developed, one that gave him a prime suspect.

Relatives of Christopher Horton told Nunez about a song called "Ride Out" that a local rapper named Antwain Steward (who performed under the stage name Twain Gotti) had written and produced a YouTube video for. Steward and Horton were allegedly members of rival gangs, and at one point they had gotten into a fight. The song,

Horton's relatives claimed, was Steward's account of his revenge, particularly the following lines:

> Listen, walked to your boy and I approached him
> Twelve midnight on his traphouse porch and
> Everybody saw when I motherfuckin' choked him
> But nobody saw when I motherfuckin' smoked him
> Roped him, sharpened up the shank then I poked him
> .357 Smith & Wesson beam scoped him, roped him.[1]

On its face, the verse is teeming with depictions of violence that are almost comically exaggerated. In a mere six lines, the unnamed victim ("your boy") is choked, then shot ("smoked"), then choked again (this time "roped"), then stabbed with a shank, then shot again (by a .357 Magnum handgun), then "roped" one last time for good measure. As *Washington Post* reporter Alyssa Rosenberg put it, the song "sounds more like he is describing an attempt to kill an adversary with a Rasputin-like resilience than an actual person."[2] But Nunez, eager to solve the case, looked past all the hyperbole, not to mention the lyrics that were factually inconsistent with the crime: There were two murders, not one. They didn't happen anywhere near midnight. They didn't involve choking of any sort. Nobody was stabbed. And the shell casings recovered from the scene didn't come from a .357 Magnum.

Unmoved by these details, Nunez focused with laser-like precision on the lyrics that seemed to correspond to the crime—the mention of a porch and a shooting—and when he did, he heard the confession he had been waiting for. On July 9, 2013, Steward was arrested for both murders, and during the initial interrogation that night, Detective Nunez seemed convinced that he'd just found a crucial piece of evidence that would solve the crime once and for all.[3] With Steward sitting across the table, wearing a black T-shirt and baseball cap, Nunez began reciting the lyrics line by line, pausing along the way for dramatic effect. His voice brimming with the confidence of a cat that has just cornered a mouse, he then proclaimed, "You described the murder. You talk about the murder." For Nunez, there was no distinction to be made between rap and reality. He had all he needed.

Steward's arrest, which came six years after the murders of Horton and Dean, marked a dramatic change of fortune for the young performer. By then, the twenty-two-year-old Steward had begun to make a name for himself. To his fans, he was Twain Gotti, a rapper whose tales of violence and drug dealing had begun to get attention up and down the East Coast. At the time of his arrest, he had just signed with a New York–based management group and was scheduled to begin a twenty-two-city tour—successes that he attributed to putting in eighteen hours a day, every day, to move his career forward.

To police, Steward was a gang member who had previously been convicted of a concealed weapons charge and a marijuana possession charge. They were keenly aware of his rap career as well, but they believed he was still very much embroiled in the kinds of street violence that were typical in his neighborhood. What's worse, he was now openly bragging about criminal exploits in his rap songs, perhaps believing that his growing fame made him untouchable to the authorities, much like his namesake, John Gotti, the notorious head of New York's Gambino crime family.

And so, with the so-called confession from "Ride Out" at the center of their investigation, police began building their case against Steward. Without any physical evidence to work with, Detective Nunez "developed" new eyewitnesses. One was an elderly neighbor of Horton's who, five years after the shooting, claimed that she saw a "light-skinned" African American man running past her house just before the shooting, brandishing a gun. She then picked Steward out of a line-up that Nunez presented to her for the first time. Steward is not light-skinned.

Another new witness, Martel Harris, was originally questioned by police as a potential suspect in the murders. At the time, he never mentioned Steward, but years later, after he had been convicted in an unrelated case, he came forward claiming that he had seen Steward commit the murder. He admitted that he was trying to shave time off his sentence in exchange for his testimony.

With a shaky case built on six lines from a rap song and questionable eyewitness testimony, prosecutors went to trial in May 2014, nearly a year after Steward's arrest and seven years after the crime occurred.

The trial lasted just three days. Surprisingly, at the last moment prosecutors didn't introduce Steward's rap lyrics at all. It's unclear why, particularly given that police had built their case around it and a judge was prepared to allow it. Perhaps prosecutors realized that the song-as-confession argument developed by gang detectives lacked credibility? Regardless, without the rap video, they had to try the case on actual evidence.

Although the predominantly white jury did find Steward guilty of gun charges, they found him not guilty of both murders. It was little comfort to Steward, who was still sentenced to sixteen years on those gun charges: a mandatory eight years for the two counts of using a firearm in the commission of a felony and another eight years on the charge of shooting into an occupied dwelling. But it was a stinging rebuke to the prosecutors, who had mounted a highly publicized murder case based on the questionable work of Newport News gang detectives. Without the highly prejudicial video to play in front of jurors, the evidence had to stand on its own. And it didn't.

Anti-gang police units are common nationwide, from large metropolitan areas to smaller cities and towns. Over the last decade, these units have moved much of their policing online, monitoring the social media accounts and online activities of young black and Latino men, often before any crime has occurred. Armed with this information, they work in tandem with prosecutors, who have become increasingly emboldened in their use of rap lyrics to secure charges and convictions.

Today's gang units—specialized units within police departments that focus on gang enforcement—are often formed in jurisdictions with a perceived gang problem as a way to indicate that police and politicians are "doing something" about it. And in the last two decades, the number of gang units has increased dramatically, particularly around 2006. According to a 2010 report by the Bureau of Justice Statistics, 365 of the country's large police departments and sheriff's offices (offices with more than a hundred officers) had specialized gang units.[4] Approximately 35 percent of those units were formed between 2004 and 2007, with more than forty created in 2006 alone.

The reasons for their creation, or their effectiveness, are not entirely clear. Research indicates that while some gang units may form in response to an actual increase in gang activity, others are formed for less palatable reasons.[5] For instance, studies have shown that police in some cities, such as Phoenix, have exaggerated, or outright invented, a "gang problem" in order to justify increased funding from local, state, and federal sources. Research also suggests that gang units are formed in response to community fears about certain minority groups, even when those fears are not borne out by actual crime statistics.[6]

Aside from the reasons for their creation, these units also raise questions about their effectiveness. They often work in isolation, both from the larger police department that houses them and, more important, the community they serve. One major study found that gang units rarely seek community input and that officers in these units have limited contact with the community or even gang members themselves.[7]

Both research and case studies reveal that gang units are primarily focused on intelligence gathering rather than, say, prevention. Today, that means they spend a *lot* of time on the Internet. According to the head of the Newport News police gang unit—the unit that built a case around Antwain Steward's YouTube video—the police in his unit spend the same amount of time browsing through social media sites and watching videos as they do on the street.[8]

That's consistent with strategies employed by gang units across the country. In 2012, New York City announced that it was doubling the size of its gang unit, to three hundred people, in order to monitor people who were allegedly boasting about their crimes or threatening one another over social media.[9] This massive increase came even as gangs accounted for less than 1 percent of city crime. The city would be deploying more gang police than there were total gang-motivated crimes (264) for that fiscal year. But with a potential treasure trove of new information to be gleaned from social media, New York was, like departments across the country, ramping up anti-gang efforts to respond to the new world of Internet-based "threats."

That begins to explain the significant uptick in rap on trial beginning in the mid-2000s. Social media use, particularly among young adults ages eighteen to twenty-nine, was exploding.[10] In 2005, just 12 percent of young adults used social media. By 2006, that number had more than tripled to 41 percent, and by 2008, it reached 63 percent. (Today that number hovers around 90 percent.)[11] With millions of young men and women suddenly online, police became aware of an entirely new universe of discourse, much of it totally foreign to them.

And police didn't understand it then any more than they do now. They saw young men talking about drugs, sex, and violence. They were holding guns—some props, but many probably real—and some were flashing gang signs. Police didn't see this as a flourishing artistic movement. Instead, they saw it as black kids who were foolishly confessing to crime or telling them where the next crime might be, as in the movie *Minority Report*. The head of the gang unit that went after Antwain Steward makes that clear enough. When asked if he considered the fictional or artistic elements of the videos he and his officers spend hours on end watching, he replied, "We are not dealing with the brightest guys," adding, "It's much easier to write about something than to think of something."[12]

To be perfectly fair about it, some of the people posting these videos *could be* talking about crimes that they have committed in the past—or they could be committing crimes in the videos themselves. Some, for example, probably should not be holding guns because state or federal law, or their own criminal records, makes it unlawful for them to do so. Many videos depict drug use or drug production. In some cases, these videos are likely created using props, but not all.

And in areas where gangs are active, you can find gang members using rap videos to taunt or threaten members of rival gangs, in a practice known as "cyberbanging." Often the battles remain rhetorical, but in some cases they can escalate to literal violence on the street. Perhaps the best-known example was the feud between nationally known rapper Chief Keef, considered "the prince of violent Chicago rap," and fellow Chicago rapper Lil JoJo, a teenager rising in the local rap scene.[13] According to police, JoJo was affiliated with a faction of the Gangster Disciples criminal street gang and he had begun to make a name for himself by posting taunts and diss tracks directed at Keef, a member of the rival Black Disciples street gang, and his crew. On September 4, 2012, JoJo confronted a friend of Keef's on the street and posted the encounter to YouTube. Within hours, JoJo was killed in a drive-by shooting.

Questionable video production methods and cyberbanging may blur the distinction between the fictional universe of rap and the violent reality of cities like Chicago. But rather than assume, as police often do, that violent rap videos are precursors to or evidence of violent crime, they—and we—might be better served by considering the opposite perspective. What if Lil JoJo's death, and other incidents of violence, occur in spite of these rap battles and not because of them?

In his book *Chicago Hustle and Flow*, scholar Geoff Harkness takes a close look at the connections between Chicago's gang culture and its hip hop culture. After spending years among the gang members themselves, he acknowledges that real violence can erupt when online rap battles become literal battles. But his findings indicate that these online exchanges often serve to diffuse violence rather than promote it. "Many gang members go out of their way to avoid physical altercations," notes Harkness. "In addition to serving as tools for marketing and recruitment, the songs and music videos were utilized as a nonviolent means by which a gang could wage battles with or disrespect adversaries, and sometimes settle disputes."[14] Consistent with the symbolic nature of hip hop battles generally, in his research Harkness concludes that "the 'dis' songs and videos brimmed with symbolic violence, but were largely a web-based phenomenon that enabled gang members to cyberbang without the threat of physical violence or arrest."[15]

We don't have to take a romanticized view here. Of course some rap battles—in person or via social media—go too far. Tempers can flare. Pride is on the line. But as a rule, they function as an alternative to violence. That police seem unwilling or unable to acknowledge this, preferring instead to view these battles as true crime being played out before their very eyes, is disingenuous. It is also dangerous. It leads to overpolicing and in some cases steep punishment for people who are attempting to keep their battles on wax (that is, confined to music).

But the persistent view among law enforcement is that rap is, in the words of Dana Griesen, San Diego's chief prosecutor for the gang division, "just another form of communication that gang members use."[16] Griesen offered this assessment as authorities in San Diego attempted the boldest, most far-reaching application of the law we've ever seen to punish a local rapper named Brandon Duncan, better known to fans as Tiny Doo.

Duncan's case dates back to 2014, when San Diego authorities charged more than a dozen people for their role in a series of gang-related shootings the previous year. Duncan was among the men charged, but his case was unique. Authorities acknowledged that Duncan had played no part in the shootings and had no knowledge that they would occur. They charged Duncan for one reason: a rap album he had created called *No Safety*. The album's lyrics didn't feature any content specifically related to the shootings in question. But prosecutors charged him with conspiracy, drawing on an infrequently used California law that makes it a felony to (1) actively participate in a criminal street gang (2) knowing that the gang or its members have engaged in a pattern of criminal activity and to (3) willfully promote, further, assist, or benefit from that activity.[17]

Essentially, prosecutors argued that Duncan was a member of the gang, even though he had long since moved away from the area where the gang was active, and even though he had no criminal record whatsoever. (He had a nine-to-five job and was supporting a family at the time.) In their estimation Duncan's music promoted the gang by glorifying violent behavior *and* he also benefitted from the gang activity by increasing his "street cred."

In March 2015, a trial judge dismissed the case against Duncan and another (a college student named Aaron Harvey who was charged based on Facebook posts), concluding the government had insufficient evidence to move forward with the case.[18] By this time, Duncan had spent almost eight months in jail because he could not afford the $500,000 bail.

Then chief prosecutor Bonnie Dumanis, showing little regret for the actions of her office, issued a statement through her spokesperson, which included the following comments:

> The District Attorney's Office respects the decision of the court today. This ruling and future court opinions will help determine if California Penal Code 182.5 is a viable legal tool in our fight against violent crime committed by San Diego street gangs across the County.
>
> In recent weeks, the District Attorney has reached out to community members, state and local legislators, and faith-based leaders, meeting with them to discuss their understandable concerns about the use of this law. While a debate over the law can be constructive and educational, combatting the scourge of deadly gang violence remains our focus. Instead of waiting for more shootings and murders to victimize the community we used this law to cripple the organization.
>
> It's unfortunate that in spite of the evidence transparently available in the court record and court's rulings that clearly establish their active gang membership during the time of the shootings, the media and community has allowed itself to be manipulated by individuals who are misrepresenting their true level of gang involvement.[19]

As the local ACLU chapter had earlier remarked, under Dumanis's interpretation of the law, her office could prosecute individuals for writing a book or making a documentary about gangs, interviewing gang members, or even being a drug abuse counselor who draws on gang experiences for his work. All of those individuals "benefit" from knowledge of gang activities.[20]

Two years later, in April 2017, Dumanis's tenure as the county's chief prosecutor ended with her resignation.[21] As she left the office, she admitted in retrospect that she had not expected to be criticized for her position on the case. But she had learned lessons about blacks and their experience of criminal justice in America by watching Ava DuVernay's movie *13th*. And she apologized, sort of.[22]

Although Duncan is free and Dumanis is gone from the prosecutor's office, the matter continues on. In January 2017, Duncan (and Harvey) filed a federal civil suit against the City of San Diego and the two officers who conducted the investigation and arrests. The suit alleged violation of the First Amendment and unlawful arrest based on a lack of probable cause.[23] They seek damages for personal loss as well as punitive damages. The case is still pending.[24]

Duncan's case sounds an alarm because it reveals the potential reach of rap on trial. Until Duncan's case, California's gang conspiracy law was rarely used in the manner it was against Duncan. If similar prosecutions are allowed to go unchecked, this sends a strong signal that criminalization of rap is permissible, regardless of trial rules aimed at fairness and constitutional principles.

And what does that mean for the future of rap and rappers? Will the criminal justice system put rap out of business by discouraging and eliminating a generation of up-and-coming and amateur rappers? How can we fix the system? How can we protect fledgling rappers? Well, we've tried, but we can't accomplish any of that without your help.

CONCLUSION

Since Andrea began looking at this issue in 2006, she has considered a number of proposals.[1] For instance, she was initially inclined toward the idea of an absolute ban on rap music evidence, given "the complexity and attention necessary for determining whether lyrics should be admissible and what weight they are due."[2] But she didn't want to elevate form over substance. She didn't want to declare that "whatever is written in the form of rap would be inadmissible" for fear of the admissibility debate shifting to a debate about whether or not particular writings could be evaluated as rap lyrics at all. So at the time she resisted what she considered an extreme remedy. She did, however, leave open the possibility that a categorical ban would be appropriate down the road. For the time, she focused her suggestions on "how best to ensure that courts and jurors fairly consider such evidence." After identifying and rejecting a couple of options, she settled on a "two-pronged approach requiring (1) a point-of-view adjustment for judicial admissibility determinations and (2) the considered use of expert testimony by both judges and jurors." You may wonder, rightly, what all that means.

Let's just say that once her article was published, the result was kind of like an album in the old days. Only one song became a hit. The solution that eventually became popular was the one that allowed defendants confronted with rap lyric evidence to call an expert witness to testify on the "composition of and societal response to rap music lyrics." The expert might opine that "rap music lyrics are subject to interpretive ambiguity, are ubiquitous, constitute braggadocio, and are fantastical or fictional . . . [rather than] autobiographical confessions of the crime charged, or an expression of mindset." Or an expert could "reveal the character-based and inflammatory nature of rap music lyrical evidence."

This proposal was moderate, seeking to even out the legal landscape by giving the government and defense equal access to tools when arguing over the introduction of the evidence. The idea was that if prosecutors could have government experts testify as to the meaning of lyrics, then defendants were equally entitled to have experts.

Despite early resistance, this solution has apparently become generally accepted.

Defense attorneys from across the country have reached out to us for case consultation and expert referrals. Courts nationwide have approved defense expert testimony. In fact, in a 2017 case (*State v. Christopher Bassett*), the chief justice of the Tennessee Supreme Court ruled that providing an expert on rap music was "necessary for the protection of the Constitutional rights" of the defendant under both the U.S. Constitution and the Constitution of the State of Tennessee.

Eventually, Erik burst on the scene, became one of those experts, formed a partnership with Andrea, the problem was solved, and the rest was history. Not so fast. Erik burst on the scene, became one of those experts, formed a partnership with Andrea, and here they are years later together tackling a practice that has invaded the criminal justice process rather than withered under scrutiny.

The problem is growing because solutions thus far have been inadequate.

Yes, there have been bright spots. Erik has offered expert testimony, for example, that has been very effective for defendants. Take the case of Anthony Murillo, a young man from Santa Maria, California. In 2013, Murillo—a teenager at the time—was accused of making a threat after he wrote a rap song with violent rhetoric that was directed at two high school girls, who were named in the song. Erik was one of the few witnesses called by the defense—the only expert—and his job was to educate the predominantly white jury on rap, a genre that many admitted (after the trial) they didn't like or understand.

In 2017, when the case was finally tried, the jury came back with a full acquittal. When asked in post-trial interviews about their decision, jurors highlighted the importance of Erik's testimony. One juror noted that the testimony was key to her decision because it "put the defendant's behavior into perspective" for her and others. She claimed that she came away from it realizing that the defendant's intent was not to threaten the girls, but to write a "bitchin'" (her word) rap song. Other jurors made similar comments.

Erik has had other successes, suggesting that an expert really can be important. But just as often, his testimony doesn't alter the outcome in ways that can be measured. He has watched multiple people he testified for get sentenced to life in prison. One man, Ronnie Fuston of Oklahoma, was sentenced to death despite his efforts during the sentencing phase.

And these are just the cases Erik has been involved with. The reality is that there aren't enough experts to go around given the scope of rap on trial, and what's more, most defense attorneys don't even think to contact one. They go to trial with no meaningful ability to challenge the characterizations made by the prosecutor and police expert. Predictably, that doesn't usually end well.

Expert testimony may help, but it's not going to solve this. The way to protect defendants is to keep the lyrics out of court altogether. Below, we offer specific suggestions for achieving that, but one of the most basic things we can do is publicize the practice. When Erik first learned about the use of rap as evidence and wondered why nobody had blown it up in the media, that's what he started to do. Over the last several years he has written op-eds and other pieces for the *New York Times, Washington Post, Rolling Stone, USA Today, Atlantic, Vox,* and others. He brought the issue to multiple television networks, including *PBS NewsHour,* which did a full segment on it.

In fact, that *NewsHour* segment featured the case of Antwain Steward, which we discussed in Chapter 6. Prosecutors had signaled that they were going to introduce his rap video(s) against him, so in concert with Steward's attorney, Erik notified media outlets across the country, and many covered the case, in the process raising questions about the fairness of using rap as evidence. As the trial was set to begin, police and prosecutors in Newport News were fielding calls from media outlets as far away as Germany.

When the trial began, Erik was in a nearby hotel room, waiting to be called to testify. That call never came. The prosecutors had blinked. In the face of his testimony, as well as the media spotlight, they decided not to introduce any rap lyrics at all. It's very possible that Steward, who was acquitted of the most serious charges (murder), would've been found guilty if those lyrics had been admitted. Because of that outcome and others, publicity has proven itself to be valuable. We need more people to know that this is happening in their communities. We hope that as rap on trial becomes more widely known, it will wither under the same scrutiny as it did in Newport News.

Beyond quality defense expert testimony and publicity, what can be done to stop rap on trial? Some ideas are ambitious, to put it mildly. But they are worth envisioning, if only to offer a pathway for change in the long term. Others are more achievable measures that can be taken by those who work within the criminal justice system, or you, the reader.

There is no magic-bullet solution to stopping rap on trial. Trust us. We wanted to come up with one. We tried. We have brainstormed for weeks, months, years. We generated lists. We worked through the proposals. Some were ambitious. Others were small but, we hoped, impactful. We added ideas. We deleted ideas. We talked. We fought—politely, of course. We compromised. (One thing we did not do is battle rap, out of respect for battle rap.) Here's where we landed, starting with the big ideas.

Rap shield rules. Given that other measures we've tried haven't led to the end of rap on trial, we propose legislators nationwide enact rap shield rules that completely ban the use of rap lyrics, videos, or promotional materials as evidence in criminal proceedings. We realize that convincing legislators to support such a broad rule would be a heavy lift politically. We ourselves do not agree on whether there are sufficient legal justifications for broadly curtailing rap as evidence in criminal cases. And certainly we aren't naïve enough to believe that elected officials would be willing to risk their jobs on this issue. But we still propose it because we don't believe that the criminal justice system has the tools or willingness to set reasonable boundaries. As a group, judges haven't shown themselves capable of applying the rules of evidence thoughtfully when it comes to rap music. They've been unwilling to educate themselves on the nuance and sophistication in hip hop, even as it has become the most influential musical genre of the last half century. And they've deferred to the "expertise" of law enforcement professionals with absolutely no expertise. We don't trust the gatekeeping they provide, and we certainly don't expect prosecutors to limit themselves. So until our justice system is better equipped to handle evidence that is biased and stereotypical, one option is to keep it out altogether.

Expressive speech privileges. In addition to rap shield rules, we also support legislative rules limiting the use of evidence that receives First Amendment protection. This is not out of order. As a matter of social policy, rules uniformly exclude helpful evidence if admitting it would undermine the open communication desired in some privileged relationships (e.g., the privileges attaching to communications between attorneys and clients, therapists and patients, and spouses). Excluding rap lyrics because allowing them to be used in the courtroom would chill constitutionally protected speech seems like a good enough reason to add it to the list of social policies trumping the goals of the criminal legal process.

Rigorous judicial oversight. Blanket rules about evidence that should and should not be permissible are obviously ambitious. We admit they may be unrealistic goals, particularly in the short term. But as another way to limit rap lyrics evidence, we call on judges to more aggressively perform their gatekeeping function when qualifying government experts who will testify regarding rap lyrics and music. Judicial oversight would be improved with topical training and a willingness to seek outside, independent expertise.

To support its arguments admitting rap lyrics as criminal evidence, the government is not relying on experts in music, literature, popular culture, linguistics, or African American studies. Rather, prosecutors routinely use law enforcement officers as experts, and these officers lack education or knowledge in the field of rap music. For their part, judges are freely permitting this expert testimony rather than acting as gatekeeper. And this happens even though defense attorneys challenge the witnesses, seeking to exclude their testimony.

Judges are specifically tasked with ensuring that any expert for any party has the necessary qualifications, training, and sound methodology to offer information or an opinion.[3] Yet they regularly fail. They willingly accept that a police officer has the appropriate credentials to interpret words and opine on the meaning of lyrics rather than make the riskier decision to exclude the evidence because the state's expert is actually ill-equipped to serve as one. They reason that the jury can decide whether to believe or discredit the evidence due to deficiencies in the officer's credentials or testimony. Sometimes, though, the court should just make the decision to exclude the evidence instead of passing off the responsibility to jurors.[4]

To assist them with performing their gatekeeping role, we suggest that judges receive training on this practice at "judge school." Judges are often members of professional organizations and attend trainings and annual meetings. Meeting organizers can and should add this topic to the agenda. The training should emphasize understanding the history, artistry, and industry of rap music, as well as the social science of rap. It should not be through the lens of gang policing or prosecution.

In addition to judicial training that would be helpful in resolving questions of admissibility, we believe that judges should seek out their own expert witness to provide testimony on behalf of the court. A court-appointed expert could provide information to the judge making the admissibility ruling. And if the judge admits the evidence, the expert can inform the jury. Judges have long had discretion to appoint experts. The federal rules of evidence specifically permit a court to appoint an expert witness on its own motion, regardless of whether either party has an expert witness.[5] Using this tool, the court can independently control the quality of the court's expert witness and the scope of the testimony. That's a big, but achievable, first step.

We acknowledge that some of our proposals face long odds and would take time and significant resources to implement. But what can *you* do, on your own, in the near term? Here are some ideas.

Nullify. We recommend that if you find yourself seated as a juror on a case involving rap lyrics, refuse to use the evidence in making your decision. Decide the case without the rap music evidence. Ignore the evidence wholesale, and reject any related testimony or opinion from the government's law enforcement witness. You can do this even while still considering all the other evidence in assessing whether the defendant is innocent or guilty.

You might be wondering: "Can I do that? Won't I get in trouble?" Our emphatic response is "Yes! Yes, you can!" and "No. No, you won't."

Jurors are constitutionally responsible for evaluating the evidence in a criminal jury trial. Jurors determine the facts, apply the facts to the law as instructed by the judge, and determine guilt or innocence.[6] Hence, as a constitutional matter, jurors independently decide which pieces of evidence to deem trustworthy and which to dismiss. Consistent with this constitutional duty, judges formally instruct jurors that they are finders of fact and can use their judgment in accepting or rejecting evidence as credible in whole or part.[7]

Just to be clear, you can stand alone in your thinking. It wouldn't matter if other jurors viewed the evidence as useful and wanted to use it. So long as you listen to the entire case with an open mind and follow the judge's instructions, you can dismiss the evidence for most any reason.[8]

It doesn't matter whether there is counterbalancing evidence to take its place. You can reject the evidence even if the defense has not challenged, contradicted, or undermined the evidence. Ideally the court would have found justification to categorically exclude the evidence from consideration. And if the evidence was admitted, ideally the defense attorney would have attempted to demonstrate its untrustworthiness. But neither may have happened. Even so, that does not mean you have to accept the evidence. Jurors are vested with independent authority to accept or reject evidence. The judge is merely a gatekeeper of evidence. The attorneys are simply arguing their respective, opposing cases based on the admitted evidence. The jury determines what evidence will be used to make a decision and whether there is sufficient evidence to convict.

You can reject the evidence even if the defense has not expressly asked you to do so. Consistent with the judge's instruction that jurors are the finders of fact, defense attorneys may likely argue that you should reject or throw out that evidence during your deliberations. They will ask you to engage in evidence nullification but probably not use that term. But even if the defense attorney does not, know that you still can, regardless of whatever argument the prosecution makes as to why the rap evidence is credible and proves guilt.

You can also go a step further. While judges may tell you otherwise, you can find somebody not guilty, even when the facts support guilt, if you think the law itself (or the way it's implemented) is unjust. So if you want to send a message to prosecutors, you can draw a line. Maybe, for instance, you decide that in prosecutions of nonviolent crimes, you will automatically acquit if the state introduces rap as evidence. We are not necessarily endorsing this approach, but we are here to tell you it's legal. And it's been used before. One of the reasons certain jurisdictions where marijuana was illegal stopped bringing charges for marijuana possession is that juries simply wouldn't convict defendants, even if they were guilty. That's nullification.[9]

Pick your judges and prosecutors. Support elected prosecutors and judges who have a progressive record and agenda. If you didn't know or remember, a large number of local prosecutors and judges are elected by citizens. So we decide who makes the first decisions about whether rap will be used in criminal cases. Choose wisely. Here's a rough blueprint of how to do this.

- *Identify the elected prosecutors and judges in your locale, determine the next time they are up for election, and then investigate their professional and personal backgrounds.* You may not find much. Some like to remain invisible, although they are public servants with public authority who answer to the public. Some basic questions:
  - Were they ever a public defender? Did they ever represent a criminal defendant for free?
  - Do they give to public interest organizations? Which ones?
  - Have they or their (extended) family ever been a criminal defendant or crime victim?

- *Investigate their professional decisions and policies.*
  - What public statements have they made?
  - If they are already in the position, what press releases has their office issued?
  - Have they ever dealt with rap as criminal evidence? How?
  - Have they ever used racial epithets or imagery in their work? How?

- *Ask them questions.* If the candidate appears in a public setting, ask questions—both specific ones and general ones. You may not get answers. Candidates may claim they do not want to demonstrate bias or partiality, or claim they cannot make a decision in the abstract. But keep pressing. At a minimum they should know the law and be able to tell you what the law mandates.
  - What do they think about the practice of using rap as criminal evidence? Push them on this. Many will never have thought about this before, even though it's common practice.
  - What do they think about the use of racial epithets and imagery by police, prosecutors, judges both inside and outside the courtroom?
  - How would they handle police, prosecutorial, or judicial misconduct?
  - What is the role of police, prosecutors, and judges in undoing wrongful convictions or mass incarceration?
  - How do they protect the rights of those who are vulnerable, marginalized, and underresourced?

- *Figure out whether they are running opposed.* If the candidate is running opposed, do all the above for the other candidate(s). If the candidate is running unopposed, find a progressive opponent to enter the race this time or in the next cycle. Ignore all those who tell you progressive candidates are soft on crime, don't care about victims, and will decrease public safety. Being tough on crime has gotten us nowhere fast. Find like-minded groups and organizations to support you in this work.[10]

- *Vote for the candidate with the progressive vision.* When in doubt, pick the former public defender or pro bono, publicly funded criminal defense attorney. Don't rely on political affiliation, although that may be a decent barometer if you have no other information.

- *Hold them accountable.*[11]

- *Repeat.*

Do this now. Don't wait.

Over the last handful of years, a wave of momentum has been building. Voters nationwide have elected progressive or reform-minded district attorneys in a host of localities, including Brooklyn, New York; Chicago, Illinois; Corpus Christi, Texas; Ferguson, Missouri; Houston, Texas; Orlando, Florida; and Philadelphia, Pennsylvania.[12] And the wave is spreading. As we write, progressive candidates nationwide are running closely contested races.[13]

Start now. Join the movement. Together, let's change who makes the front-line decisions about rap on trial.

EPILOGUE

West Coast, 2018. Sixteen-year-old Elijah was a high school senior.[1] He was a good student, on track to graduate a year early. He and his father had begun making college visits. He played a couple of instruments and made music. He hoped to get into a good music program somewhere.

Elijah wasn't native to the exclusive town where he lived with his parents. His parents had moved the family there a couple of years earlier. He was an outsider and a little bit awkward. It took him a while to adjust. But he leveraged his talents to do so: writing and performing rap music and posting his creations online. He was talented, and so he developed a pretty good following among his peers. His popularity increased. All that helped smooth his transition.

Another thing that helped was finding someone who could hook him up with some good marijuana. When he first got to town, a classmate told him he could get some from John,[2] another classmate. Elijah contacted John through Snapchat. The two met up, but Elijah thought John was trying to pull a fast one and sell him some weak stuff. So he didn't buy any. And he said so on Snapchat. Over the next couple of years, Elijah and John bumped into each other a few times around town. They weren't friends, but they ran in some of the same circles and saw each other at parties. Their mutual friends knew they didn't really get along. At one party in early 2018, Elijah and a classmate each separately caught John trying to steal small personal items from them, like a vape pen and hoodie. Each of them confronted John, who—not surprisingly—didn't take it well.

A couple of months later, police unexpectedly executed an arrest warrant for Elijah at his house. They also had a warrant to search his home. The charges: robbery, residential burglary, assault, conspiracy, battery, and dissuading a witness from testifying. Elijah's brother was also charged. In short, the allegations were that on Saturday, March 17, 2018, Elijah and his nineteen-year-old brother snuck into the apartment where John lived with his older brother and stole a PlayStation at knifepoint. Elijah was additionally alleged to have assaulted John with the knife, causing injury to his chest, and to have warned John not to call the police. Elijah's brother is alleged to have jumped and assaulted John's brother after being chased from the scene.

The initial allegations in the police report and as presented by the prosecutor sounded pretty serious. At his first court hearing, the juvenile court judge ordered that Elijah be detained in a juvenile facility while the case was pending.

Elijah and his brother both denied all charges and maintained their innocence. The day of the alleged incident, they had been hanging out with each other and some friends. They had not done anything like what was alleged. For Elijah's older brother, who was charged as an adult, the risk was great. So, as is common every day in the criminal legal system, he took a plea deal rather than risk a lengthy sentence if he went to trial and lost, which usually happens even if one is innocent. Elijah's situation was better, as his case stayed in juvenile court. He faced stiff punishment if found to have committed the charges. But the exposure was more manageable. So, almost two months after his arrest, he went to trial.

The facts that came out at the adjudication hearing told a very different story from what was initially alleged. According to John's testimony, Elijah had been to John's apartment before. The door was unlocked when Elijah arrived. There was no big commotion. The alleged knife attack, if it even happened, was at best a light poke with a very small knife through John's clothing. The claimed injury may actually have been a scabbed pimple. John wanted the cases to go away.

It was apparent John had not been fully truthful with the police and was not being fully truthful on the witness stand. He was holding something back.

John's older brother, a much more credible witness, admitted he couldn't identify Elijah to the police and couldn't identify who had jumped him. But that day in the courtroom it was easy for him to identify Elijah as being involved in the incident. He as much as admitted that he picked out Elijah because he was the only black person in the room. It's true—at his trial, Elijah was the only black person in the courtroom, in addition to being the only one wearing orange clothing and the only one sitting next to defense counsel. His family was there. But picking Elijah was still a no-brainer. Although Elijah and his brother are black, the two boys were adopted. Their parents and sisters are white. Their parents were there and had hired a good attorney to be by Elijah's side. He was one of a kind, an outsider, alone, but not by himself.

Elijah took the stand and told his story. He didn't evade. He didn't minimize. He didn't waffle. Quite simply: He wasn't there. He didn't do it.

Based on the evidence, the case was weak. Something had happened to John and his brother, but it was highly debatable whether Elijah and his brother had done it, and whatever happened was certainly not as serious as it had been made to sound.

The prosecutor had to shore up what was turning into a weak case, and she turned to rap. While he was detained, Elijah had had lots of downtime, so he did what he does to cope and pass the time: he wrote. Lots. He wrote in a journal, which the prosecutor got hold of. In less than two months he had written sixty-plus pages of rap lyrics. A small sample size included:

"I'll murk yuh"
"cut you up like el chapo"
"I prolly wanna fight yuh. My nigga gon ignite yuh"
"AK with a beam. Chopper wid a scope"
"got me locked up"
"was up in juvenile hall. Had to beat my case,"
"ballin cuz I did the race tay k, keep a k. KKK like my chopper hate niggas"
"try and snitch on me. I was tryna beat my case."

With no basis other than a personal reading of the lyrics, the prosecutor argued the lyrics were confessions to the charged crimes, were evidence of motive (promotion of a hard image), revealed a lack of remorse and avoidance of personal accountability, and demonstrated an anti-snitching ethos. Elijah's defense counsel countered that the lyrics were fiction and art, inspired by what Elijah was going through but not true to life. He also mentioned that Elijah had received class credit for his writings.

After reviewing them and considering the attorneys' arguments, the court excluded the lyrics, finding their little relevance to the case to be outweighed by the prejudice they would cause, and viewing them as inadmissible character evidence. Small victory. The court found Elijah responsible on two of the charges and dismissed the other four, rejecting the charges that alleged violence or assault. About a month later, at the hearing to determine what his punishment would be, the court reversed course and relied on the lyrics when issuing its decision.

In preparation for the hearing to set his punishment, Elijah's attorney had done what is considered best practice. He obtained character letters regarding Elijah from his family and family friends. The court recognized the letters, remarking that the letters described Elijah as "polite, kind, sweet, and respectful." The court then contrasted those letters with his rap lyrics, commenting that the letters contrasted with the "extremely dark side . . . that is reflected in his writings and which cannot be ignored."

The court viewed the lyrics as "glamorizing crime" and as reflective of his self-perception "as a criminal." Finally, the court pointed to a lyric mentioning the fictional movie character Rambo: "You compared yourself to Rambo, going through the house like an assassin. . . . [T]he Court did find it chilling, because you had gone into a house armed." (You judge how that conclusion compared to the questionable testimony by John.) Needless to say, the court's decision on punishment was not favorable. The court committed Elijah to the custody of the state for one year, rather than returning him home on supervision.

Without sustained intervention aimed at ending rap on trial, Elijah and others like him are the future targets of prosecutors wielding rap as evidence. The injustices in our criminal system are in many ways facilitated and reproduced by institutions charged with the welfare of our children. Not only are young men fed through the criminal justice system because of their music, but out of the public eye, children are disciplined for the same thing, whether in schools or in juvenile court. The consequences may be less severe for them than for someone in a criminal context, but they are children: any exposure to "the system" promises to be life-altering, and it paves the way to further, more serious trouble with the authorities down the road.

We have a number of goals for the coming years, all of them intended to provide resources for those working to reverse rap on trial. Here are a few:

Experts. We want to increase the number of experts who are qualified to provide testimony—and who are willing to do so. There's no shortage of people in the academy, for example, who are qualified to serve as experts in these cases. The problem is that many people are reluctant to do it. Academics in particular are not accustomed to having their ideas challenged by a determined, adversarial prosecutor whose goal is to win a case instead of to represent scholarly ideas in all their nuance. It can be nerve-racking. In addition, defense attorneys are reluctant to put a first-time expert on the stand.

We plan to address both sides of the problem by creating workshops in which we invite potential experts to work with experienced lawyers, judges, and experts to learn some basic strategies for testifying: how to answer questions effectively, how to handle a confrontational cross examination, and how to make complex information accessible to the layperson.

We also hope to secure funding so that even if defense attorneys don't have the resources to pay an expert, they can still benefit from one.

Defense resources. We are in the process of creating a set of resources for defense attorneys whose clients may have their rap lyrics used against them. Among those resources will be a step-by-step guide that offers strategies for attorneys at all stages of the process, from arrest to post-conviction sentencing. Along with that, we are organizing materials we've received from our research—sample briefs, names of qualified experts, and contact information for defense attorneys who have defended these cases before (and who are willing to provide guidance). We also plan to provide some of the primary research presented here, much of which is hidden behind publisher paywalls. (We will of course observe all copyright laws in doing so.)

Research. The research on rap on trial is growing, and we plan to keep adding to it ourselves. The greatest obstacle to research, however, is the legal system itself. Collectively, courts are terribly inconsistent with respect to making their records accessible. What shows up in legal databases such as Westlaw is more of a smattering of cases than a thorough record. That makes it very difficult for us to track cases involving rap music. While we want to see more transparency across the board, we're not waiting. We plan to identify two or three key jurisdictions and conduct a sustained search for records, hoping to get a sense of the breadth and scope of the problem in those areas. This, we believe, is a practical way to gain a better understanding of how this process is working at the local level.

Industry. We hope to engage the music industry. With some notable exceptions—Michael Render (aka Killer Mike) foremost among them—artists and industry executives have been surprisingly quiet about this. That is slowly changing with efforts such as the March 2019 amicus (friend-of-the-court) brief that was filed in the case of Jamal Knox, the young man from Pittsburgh who was convicted of making terroristic threats toward police officers. In support of his case, and the right to freedom of expression more broadly, a number of well-known artists—including Atlanta rappers Killer Mike and 21 Savage, Chicago artist Chance the Rapper, Philadelphia rapper Meek Mill, and Luther Campbell of 2 Live Crew—submitted a brief urging the U.S. Supreme Court to overturn Knox's conviction and to affirm that rap music is indeed worthy of First Amendment protections.[3]

Even though they weren't successful in Knox's case, these efforts are important. We believe that the hip hop industry (and the larger music industry) should be speaking out about this—not only because it's the right thing to do but also because we see the potential for real liability if courts continue to read rap lyrics literally. If they are deemed confessions to crime, incitements to violence, true threats, or defamation, it won't be long before artists, record labels, radio stations, and television networks find themselves explaining, in the media or court, why they are knowingly producing and distributing such content. We think it's smarter for them to get in front of the problem, and we plan to help them see their interest.

It's in the interest of all of us to have a justice system that works fairly. It's in the interest of all of us to live in a country that protects speech, art, expression. And it's in the interest of all of us to confront the profound inequalities embedded in our systems of power. Rap on trial is just one example, but we view it as the proverbial loose thread. Our hope is that if we pull it, we can begin the long-overdue process of unwinding a justice system that is anything but just.

ACKNOWLEDGMENTS

This is the hardest part of the book for me. So many have contributed to this project over the years, and undoubtedly I will forget someone. If I leave you out, my bad. Please know it was accidental, and I couldn't have done it without you.

A big shout-out to family and friends who encouraged and supported me on this journey, particularly my husband, Keith, and son, Reed, who put up with me in the day-to-day. I know it wasn't easy.

This project is rooted in my earlier life as an assistant federal public defender. My colleagues in that office were among the best lawyers I have ever worked with. Much respect to all those who battle every day on the front lines. And to all those in cages, I see you.

Scholars Tricia Rose, Imani Perry, and Paul Butler inspired me. Much respect.

The Mid-Atlantic Criminal Law Research Collective has been ride-or-die from the beginning. Thanks for being on my side.

I am indebted to my former colleagues at the University of Kentucky College of Law who nurtured my original article on this phenomenon. My current academic home, the University of Georgia School of Law, fostered this extended treatment by offering much-needed support, feedback, and funding. Participants in the 2018 UGA-Emory Law Workshop shared helpful insights.

Many former students provided invaluable research assistance along the way, including: Xavier Brown, Cassidy Grunninger, Madison Hahn, Matthew Lester, Jean Goetz Mangan, Ashley McGinley, and Phillips Stone Workman. My administrative assistants, Tina Whitehair and Cyndi Canup, kept me afloat throughout the process.

Katie Zanecchia, formerly of Ross-Yoon Literary Agency, believed in this project from the get go. Thanks for your guidance and enthusiasm. And thanks to Harold Yoon for stepping in to help us finish when Katie moved on to new endeavors.

I am extremely flattered that The New Press picked us. Gratitude to everyone there, especially Jed Bickman (one of our editors who went west coast before we finished), zakia henderson-brown (our editor), and Sue Warga (our copyeditor). zakia, we pushed back and so did you. The book is much the better for it. Mad props to you.

Erik, this has become so much more than a book. 'Nuff said.

—*Andrea L. Dennis*

First, I'd like to acknowledge my family, whose support has made this work, and this book, possible. In particular, I'd like to thank Sandra Park, my soon-to-be wife, for everything she has done to support me, as well as for the work she does every day as a civil rights attorney. I also want to thank my sons, Sam and Mac, for being as understanding and encouraging as they have been, even when it has meant that their dad is spending hours focusing on somebody else's son.

In addition, I would like to thank the many people at the University of Richmond who have helped me along the way, including Jim Narduzzi, Dan Roberts, Roger Skalbeck, Porcher Taylor, and Jamelle Wilson. I also want recognize the following students, whose research contributed in significant ways to this book: Lisa Cheney, Tracy Ellerman, Zach Grossfeld, Dean Liverman, Laini Marshall, and Kimberly Payne.

I am also grateful to Michael Render (aka Killer Mike), who has helped me elevate this work over the last several years. I appreciate his support and I am proud to call him a friend.

Finally, to everyone at The New Press and Ross Yoon Agency who helped make this project a reality, thank you.

—*Erik Nielson*

NOTES

Introduction

1. Paul A. Jargowsky, "Ghetto Poverty Among Blacks in the 1980s," *Journal of Policy Analysis and Management* 13, no. 2 (Spring 1994): 288–310.

2. Greg Whitt, "In 1988 Master P and No Limit Had One of the Greatest Years in Hip-Hop History," Genius.com, June 14, 2018, https://genius.com/a/in-1998-master-p-no-limit-had-one-of-the-greatest-years-in-hip-hop-history.

3. DJ Vlad, "Mac of No Limit on Serving 30 Years for Manslaughter, Lyrics Used in Trial," VladTV, July 7, 2016, https://www.youtube.com/watch?v=uBx-qdP-uJ0.

4. Neil Strauss, "How a Gangsta Rapper Turns Entrepreneur: At 28, Master P Has Created One of the Biggest Independent Labels," *New York Times*, May 13, 1998.

5. Mark Borden et al., "America's Forty Richest Under Forty," *Fortune*, September 27, 1999.

6. DJ Vlad, "Flashback: Boosie's Negative Stories with Baton Rouge Police," VladTV, March 27, 2018, https://www.youtube.com/watch?v=cb-AY40sKQ98.

7. David Lohr, "Witnesses: DA Bullied Testimony That Put Rapper Away for 30 Years," *Huffington Post*, March 18, 2015 (updated December 6, 2017).

8. Lohr, "Witnesses: DA Bullied Testimony."

9. Lohr, "Witnesses: DA Bullied Testimony."

10. Cindy Chang, "Louisiana Incarcerated (2012)," eight-part series, *Times-Picayune*, https://www.nola.com/crime/index.ssf/page/louisiana_prison_capital.html.

11. Thomas Aiello, *Jim Crow's Last Stand: Nonunanimous Criminal Jury Verdicts in Louisiana* (Baton Rouge: Louisiana State University Press, 2015). On November 6, 2018, voters in Louisiana voted to overturn the rule. Julia O'Donoghue and Heather Nolan, "Louisiana Approves Unanimous Jury Requirement, Scrapping Jim Crow–Era Law," *Times-Picayune*, November 6, 2018.

12. David Lohr, "Prosecutor Used Hip-Hop as a Weapon to Convict Mac Phipps," *Huffington Post*, March 24, 2015 (updated December 6, 2017).

13. David Lohr, "Witnesses Recant Testimony That Put Rapper C-Murder Away for Life," *Huffington Post*, July 3, 2018.

14. KC Orcutt, "21 Times Rappers Provided the Soundtrack to TV Commercials," *XXL*, July 19, 2016.

15. Pulitzer Prizes, "The 2018 Pulitzer Prize Winner in Music: *DAMN.*, by Kendrick Lamar," https://www.pulitzer.org/winners/kendrick-lamar.

16. See, e.g., New Earth, providing arts, educational, and vocational programs to system-involved youth and young adults, founded by Harry Grammer, https://newearthlife.org; Get Free Hip Hop Civics Ed, "a multimedia Hip Hop civics curriculum for youth and young adults," created by Bettina Love, Ph.D., http://getfreehiphopcivics.com; #HipHopEd, providing "Hip-Hop based interventions in STEM, therapy, literacy and school leadership," created by Christopher Emdin, Ph.D., http://hiphoped.com.

17. Susan Hadley and George Yancy, *Therapeutic Uses of Rap and Hip Hop* (Abingdon, UK: Routledge, 2011).

18. Lester Spence, *Stare into the Darkness: The Limits of Hip-hop and Black Politics* (Minneapolis: University of Minnesota Press, 2011), 69–71. For a much broader discussion of hip hop in politics, both in the United States and abroad, see Travis L. Gosa and Erik Nielson, eds., *The Hip Hop and Obama Reader* (New York: Oxford University Press, 2015).

19. *Dunn v. State*, 206 so.3d 803 (Fla. 2016); "Loud Music Murder Trial: Michael Dunn Testifies," ABC News Nightline (Feb. 12, 2014).

20. John Eligon, "Michael Brown Spent Last Weeks Grappling with Problems and Progress," *New York Times*, August 24, 2014.

21. The mothers of Jordan Davis (Lucy McBath) and Michael Brown (Lesley McSpadden) have since stepped into the political stage. Jordan's mother ran for U.S. Congress and won. Caroline Kelly, "Georgia Democrat Lucy McBath Beats GOP Rep. Karen Handel Following Tight Race," CNN, November 8, 2018. Michael's mother ran for Ferguson City Council, but lost the election in 2019. Nicole Chavez, "Michael Brown's Mother Is Running for Office in Ferguson, Missouri. Here's Why," CNN, August 11, 2018.

22. *Neblett v. Commonwealth*, 2014 WL 3714372 (Ct. of App. Of Ky. July 25, 2014).

23. Marjorie Hernandez, "Rap Expert Testifies in Ojai Valley Murder Trial," *Ventura County Star*, October 4, 2013.

24. Richard Wolf, "Supreme Court Wants to Hear Case on Facebook Threats," *USA Today*, June 16, 2014.

25. Brief for the Petitioner, *Elonis v. United States*, Supreme Court of the United States, No. 13-983, February 14, 2014.

26. Richard Wolf, "Supreme Court Wants to Hear Case on Facebook Threats," *USA Today*, June 16, 2014.

27. Alan Jackson, *Prosecuting Gang Cases: What Local Prosecutors Need to Know* (Arlington, VA: American Prosecutors Research Institute, 2004), 15–16 (emphasis added).

28. Jackson, *Prosecuting Gang Cases*, 16 (emphasis added).

29. For more on the way that listeners perceive sexually explicit content in rap as more offensive than similarly explicit content in other genres, see Travis Dixon and Daniel Linz, "Obscenity Law and Sexually Explicit Rap Music: Understanding the Effects of Sex, Attitudes, and Beliefs." *Journal of Applied Communication Research* 25, no. 3 (1997): 217–41.

30. John Knefel, "Grand Jury Rejects Indictment of Teen Arrested for Rap Lyrics," *Rolling Stone*, June 6, 2013.

31. *State v. Skinner*, 95 A.3d 236 (N.J. 2014).

32. *Amicus* Brief on Behalf of the ACLUNJ, *New Jersey v. Skinner*, Supreme Court of New Jersey, No. A-57/58-12 (071764), July 29, 2013.

33. The Sentencing Project, "Criminal Justice Facts," https://www.sentencingproject.org/criminal-justice-facts (last visited November 5, 2018).

34. Ashley Nellis, "The Color of Justice: Racial and Ethnic Disparity in State Prisons," The Sentencing Project, June 14, 2016; Federal Bureau of Prisons, "Inmate Race," https://www.bop.gov/about/statistics /statistics_inmate_race.jsp (last visited November 5, 2018).

35. Peter Wagner and Wendy Sawyer, "Mass Incarceration: The Whole Pie 2018," Prison Policy Initiative, March 14, 2018, https://www .prisonpolicy.org/reports/pie2018.html.

36. The Sentencing Project, "Criminal Justice Facts."

37. Nielsen, "2017 U.S. Music Year-End Report," January 3, 2018, https://www.nielsen.com/us/en/insights/reports/2018/2017-music-us -year-end-report.html.

38. For a broader discussion of how hip hop has been, and continues to be, used as a way to escape violence and gang life, see Jooyoung Lee, *Blowin' Up: Rap Dreams in South Central* (Chicago: University of Chicago Press, 2016).

1. Hip Hop: From the Margins to the Mainstream

1. Martin Tolchin, "South Bronx: A Jungle Stalked by Fear, Seized by Rage," *New York Times*, January 15, 1973.

2. Tolchin, "South Bronx"; Jeff Chang, *Can't Stop, Won't Stop: A History of the Hip Hop Generation* (New York: St. Martin's Press, 2005), 13.

3. Robert Worth, "Guess Who Saved the Bronx?," *Washington Monthly* 31, no. 4 (1999).

4. Cheryl L. Keyes, *Rap Music and Street Consciousness* (Urbana: University of Illinois Press, 2002), 46.

5. Joe Flood, *The Fires* (New York: Riverhead, 2010), 160.

6. Chang, *Can't Stop, Won't Stop*, 15.

7. Joe Flood, "Why the Bronx Burned," *New York Post*, May 16, 2010.

8. Worth, "Guess Who Saved the Bronx?"

9. Worth, "Guess Who Saved the Bronx?" The phrase "malign neglect" was derived from "benign neglect," the term made famous by Daniel Patrick Moynihan, who worked for the Nixon administration before becoming a U.S. senator from New York. In 1970, while working for Nixon, Moynihan wrote a memorandum that recommended a

period of "benign neglect" with respect to racial policy in the United States. His advice was widely criticized for providing a rationalization for a laissez-faire approach to racial problems.

10. Gary Hoenig, "Turf," *New York Times*, November 4, 1973.

11. Tricia Rose, *Black Noise: Rap Music and Black Culture in Contemporary America* (Middletown, CT: Wesleyan University Press, 1994), 22.

12. Sally Banes, "Breaking," in Nelson George et al., *Fresh: Hip Hop Don't Stop* (New York: Random House, 1985), 84–86.

13. Rose, *Black Noise*, 48; Robin D. G. Kelley, *Yo Mama's Disfunktional! Fighting the Culture Wars in Urban America* (Boston: Beacon Press, 1997), 67–68.

14. "Garelick Calls for War on Graffiti," *New York Times*, May 21, 1972.

15. Joe Austin, *Taking the Train* (New York: Columbia University Press, 2001), 130; Chang, *Can't Stop Won't Stop*, 135.

16. Craig Castleman, *Getting Up: Subway Graffiti in New York* (Cambridge, MA: MIT Press, 1982), 150–51.

17. Austin, *Taking the Train*, 128–30; Chang, *Can't Stop Won't Stop*, 135.

18. Quoted in Castleman, *Getting Up*, 162.

19. Erik Nielson, "'It Could Have Been Me': The 1983 Death of a NYC Graffiti Artist," *Code Switch*, NPR, September 16, 2013.

20. Philip Shenon, "Police Beat Cuffed Man, Inquiry on Death Finds," *New York Times*, August 24, 1984.

21. Sam Roberts, "Police Brutality Charged at Forum," *New York Times*, September 20, 1983.

22. Nathan Glazer, "On Subway Graffiti in New York," *The Public Interest* 54 (1979): 3–11.

23. Glazer's commentary here anticipates John Dilulio's now famous warnings about juvenile "super-predators." See John Dilulio, "The Coming of the Super-Predators," *Weekly Standard*, November 7, 1995.

24. Amiri Baraka, "Black Art," in *The Norton Anthology of African American Literature*, 2nd ed., ed. Henry Louis Gates Jr. and Nellie McKay (New York: Norton, 2004), 1943.

25. Nelson George, *Hip Hop America* (New York: Penguin, 1998), 36.

26. Frank Owen, "Hanging Tough: Our April 1990 Interview with N.W.A.," *Spin*, April 1990.

27. Campbell Gibson and Kay Jung, "Historical Census Statistics on Population Totals by Race, 1790 to 1990, and by Hispanic Origin, 1970 to 1990, for Large Cities and Other Urban Places in the United States," Working Paper No. 56, Population Division, U.S. Census Bureau, 2005; Bob Baker, "L.A.'s Booming Auto Industry Now a Memory," *Los Angeles Times*, July 20, 1991.

28. Eithne Quinn, *Nuthin' but a "G" Thang* (New York: Columbia University Press, 2005), 45.

29. Quinn, *Nuthin' but a "G" Thang*, 48–49.

30. Robert Reinhold, "In the Middle of L.A.'s Gang Wars," *New York Times*, May 22, 1988.

31. Ira Reiner, *Gangs, Crime and Violence in Los Angeles: Findings and Proposals* (Los Angeles: Office of the District Attorney, 1992).

32. Quinn, *Nuthin' but a "G" Thang*, 50.

33. During the 1980s, crack appeared on the illicit drug market, initially in Detroit, Los Angeles, Miami, and New York.

34. Michelle Alexander, *The New Jim Crow* (New York: The New Press, 2010), 48.

35. The Sentencing Project, "California Prison Population over Time," https://www.sentencingproject.org/the-facts/#map (last accessed November 6, 2018).

36. The Sentencing Project, "California Prison Population over Time."

37. The Sentencing Project, "California Prison Population over Time."

38. Marc Mauer and Ryan S. King, "A 25-Year Quagmire: The War on Drugs and Its Impact on American Society," The Sentencing Project, September 2007, 2.

39. Marc Mauer and Tracy Huling, "Young Black Americans and the Criminal Justice System: Five Years Later," The Sentencing Project, October 1995, 1.

40. Deborah Vagins and Jesselyn McCurdy, "Cracks in the System: Twenty Years of the Unjust Federal Crack Cocaine Law," American Civil Liberties Union, October 2006, i–ii.

41. "Crips and Bloods: Made in America," *Independent Lens*, PBS, 2008.

42. Joe Domanick, "Daryl Gates' Downfall," *Los Angeles Times*, April 18, 2010.

43. "Race, Rap and the L.A.P.D.," *Frontline*, PBS, 2001.

44. Dennis Romero, "The Militarization of Police Started in Los Angeles," *LA Weekly*, August 15, 2014. See also Keith Schneider, "Daryl F. Gates, L.A.P.D. Chief in Rodney King Era, Dies at 83," *New York Times*, April 16, 2010.

45. Here Davis is of course drawing on Michel Foucault's seminal work *Discipline and Punish: The Birth of the Prison*, trans. Alan Sheridan (London: Penguin, 1975).

46. Alex Alonso, "Out of the Void: Street Gangs in Black Los Angeles," in *Black Los Angeles: American Dreams and Racial Realities*, ed. Darnell Hunt and Ana-Christina Ramon (New York: NYU Press, 2010), 159.

47. Leighton Woodhouse, "50 Years After the Riots, Watts Projects and LAPD Learn to Co-Exist," Gawker, August 11, 2015.

48. David Freed, "Police Brutality Claims Are Rarely Prosecuted: Law: Vast Majority of More Than 300 Cases in L.A. County Since 1980 Were Dismissed, Times Study Finds," *Los Angeles Times*, July 7, 1991.

49. John L. Mitchell, "The Raid That Still Haunts LA," *Los Angeles Times*, March 14, 2001.

50. Robert G. Woletz, "Technology Gives the Charts a Fresh Spin," *New York Times*, January 26, 1992.

51. Stephen Holden, "Billboard's New Charts Roil the Record Industry," *New York Times*, June 22, 1991.

52. The demand for gangsta or gangsta-inspired rap would continue into the next decade. Byron Hurt's 2006 documentary *Hip-Hop: Beyond Beats and Rhymes* explores this dynamic in detail, looking in particular at the way it caused mainstream rap to embrace misogyny and violence.

53. Steve Huey, "Biography: The Notorious B.I.G.," AllMusic.com, September 26, 2003.

54. Carl Bialik, "Is the Conventional Wisdom Correct In Measuring Hip-Hop Audience?," *Wall Street Journal*, May 5, 2005.

55. Asawin Suebsaeng, "The FBI Agent Who Hunted N.W.A," *Daily Beast*, August 14, 2015.

56. Peter Blecha, *Taboo Tunes: A History of Banned Bands and Censored Songs* (San Francisco: Backbeat Books, 2004), 128.

57. Dave Marsh and Phyllis Pollack, "Wanted for Attitude," *Village Voice*, October 10, 1989. See also Erik Nielson, "'Can't C Me': Surveillance and Rap Music," *Journal of Black Studies* 40, no. 6 (2010): 1254–74.

58. George Lipsitz, "The Hip Hop Hearings: Censorship, Social Memory, and Intergenerational Tensions Among African Americans," in *Generations of Youth: Youth Cultures and History in Twentieth-Century America*, ed. Joe Austin and Michael Willard (New York: NYU Press, 1998), 401–2.

59. Ice-T and Douglas Century, *Ice: A Memoir of Gangster Life and Redemption—From South Central to Hollywood* (New York: One World Books, 2011), 142.

60. Nicole White and Evelyn McDonnell, "Police Secretly Watching Hip Hop Artists," *Miami Herald*, March 9, 2004.

61. Jay-Z, *Decoded* (New York: Random House, 2010), 162.

62. Jay-Z, *Decoded*, 162.

63. *Something from Nothing: The Art of Rap*, dir. Ice-T and Andy Baybutt (JollyGood Films, 2012).

64. David Simon (@AoDespair), Twitter, November 2, 2017, https://twitter.com/aodespair/status/926270593904676864?lang=en.

65. *Something from Nothing: The Art of Rap*.

66. Jay-Z, *Decoded*, 54–55.

67. Henry Louis Gates Jr., "Foreword," in *The Anthology of Rap*, ed. Adam Bradley and Andrew DuBois (New Haven, CT: Yale University Press, 2010), xxv.

68. "U Dubb Presents Loaded Lux vs Hollow Da Don," U Dubb Network, July 13, 2014, https://www.youtube.com/watch?v=7q4BshCzxs.

69. Eminem on *60 Minutes*, October 10, 2010.

70. "Screw Rick Ross," The Smoking Gun, July 21, 2008.

71. "Rap Lyrics Used as Evidence in Brooklyn Murder Trial," WPIX-TV, June 5, 2014.

72. Stephanie Clifford, "Rappers' Lyrics and Lifestyles Scrutinized in Murder Case," *New York Times*, June 18, 2014.

73. *United States v. Herron*, 2019 WL 626150 (2d. Cir. Feb. 14, 2019).

74. Carlton Ridenhour and Yusuf Jah, *Fight the Power: Rap, Race, and Reality* (New York: Dell, 1997), 256.

75. Murray Forman. *The 'Hood Comes First: Race, Space, and Place in Rap and Hip Hop* (Middletown, CT: Wesleyan University Press, 2002).

76. For a discussion of lyric formulas—stock lyrical topics understood by musicians and their audiences, many of which make sense only in the context of a given genre—see Nicholas Stoia, Kyle Adams, and Kevin Drakulich, "Rap Lyrics as Evidence: What Can Music Theory Tell Us?," *Race and Justice* 8, no. 4 (2018).

2. Rap Enters the Courtroom

1. "August 6, 1991: The WWW Debuts," CNN, March 10, 2003.

2. *United States v. Foster*, 939 F.2d 445 (7th Cir. 1991).

3. *Foster* is the earliest case we have uncovered through exhaustive research. There may be an earlier case, but if so, we have been unable to locate it using publicly available sources.

4. E.g., *United States v. Recio*, 884 F.3d 230, 236 (4th Cir. 2018); *Brown v. State*, No. 1302 Sept. Term 2013, 2016 WL 5720590, at *6 (Md. Ct. Spec. App. Sept. 30, 2016).

5. *State v. Deases*, 476 N.W. 2d 91 (Iowa App. 1991).

6. *People v. Olguin*, 31 Cal.App.4th 1355 (1994).

7. *People. v. Spraggins*, 723 N.E.2d 359 (Ill. App. Ct. 1999).

8. *Britt v. State*, 974 S.W.2d 436 (Ark. 1998).

9. Michelle Garcia, "N.Y. Using Terrorism Law to Prosecute Gang Cases," *Washington Post*, February 1, 2005.

10. Ill. Comp. Stat. Ann. 5/29D-10(l).

11. Timothy Williams, "Gang Member Is Convicted Under Terror Law," *New York Times*, November 1, 2007.

12. Justin Peters, "Prosecutors Should Be Ashamed of Their Egregious 'Terrorism' Prosecution of Olutosin Oduwole," *Slate*, May 13, 2013.

13. *People v. Oduwole*, 2013 IL App (5th) 120039, 985 N.E.2d 316, 323 (2013).

14. *People v. Oduwole*, 2013 IL App (5th) 120039, 985 N.E.2d 316, 321 (2013).

15. For only seven states have we not been able to find a case: Montana, New Mexico, North Dakota, Rhode Island, South Dakota, Utah, and Wyoming. But—not to sound like a broken record—although we have not uncovered cases in those jurisdictions, we cannot say for sure that they do not exist. We just may not have found them yet.

16. E.g., *Elonis v. U.S.*, 575 U.S.___ (2015); John Knefel, "Grand Jury Rejects Indictment of Teen Arrested for Rap Lyrics," *Rolling Stone*, June 6, 2013.

17. Brief of Appellant Elsebeth Baumgartner, *State v. Baumgartner*, 2007 WL 6857663 (Ohio App. 8 Dist.).

18. Memorandum in Support of Jurisdiction of Appellant Elsebeth Baumgartner, *State v. Baumgartner*, 2009 WL 1872699 (Ohio).

19. *State v. Baumgartner*, 2009 WL 344988 (slip copy) (Ct. App. Ohio 8 Dist.)

3. Lyrics, Stereotypes, and Bias

1. *Commonwealth v. Hawkins*, No. 1184MDA2012, 2014 WL 10986149 (Sup. Ct. Penn. Feb. 7, 2014).

2. See, e.g., Fed. R. Evid. 401.

3. Fed. R. Evid. 404.

4. Michelle Alexander, *The New Jim Crow* (New York: The New Press 2010), 18.

5. Gordon Allport, *The Nature of Prejudice* (Cambridge, UK: Perseus Books, 1954).

6. Joshua Correll, Bernadette Park, Charles M. Judd, and Bernd Wittenbrink, "The Police Officer's Dilemma: Using Ethnicity to Disambiguate Potentially Threatening Individuals," *Journal of Personality and Social Psychology* 83, no. 6 (2002): 1314–29.

7. Mahzarin R. Banaji and R. Bhaskar, "Implicit Stereotypes and Memory: The Bounded Rationality of Social Beliefs," in *Memory, Brain,*

and Belief, ed. Daniel L. Schacter and Elaine Scarry (Cambridge, MA: Harvard University Press, 2000), 139–75.

8. Jennifer Eberhardt, Paul G. Davies, Valerie J. Purdie-Vaughns, and Sheri Lynn Johnston, "Looking Deathworthy: Perceived Stereotypicality of Black Defendants Predicts Capital-Sentencing Outcomes," *Psychological Science* 17, no. 5 (May 2006): 383–86.

9. Glenn R. Schmitt, Louis Reedt, and Kevin Blackwell, "Demographic Differences in Sentencing: An Update to the 2012 *Booker* Report," U.S. Sentencing Commission, November 2017, 2.

10. Stuart Fischoff, "'Gangsta' Rap and a Murder in Bakersfield," *Journal of Applied Social Psychology* 29, no. 4 (1999): 795–805.

11. Fischoff, "'Gangsta' Rap," 803.

12. Diane Pecknold, *The Selling Sound: The Rise of the Country Music Industry* (Durham, NC: Duke University Press, 2007).

13. Pecknold, *The Selling Sound*.

14. David Peisner, "Rhymes from the Backwoods: The Rise of Country Rap," *Rolling Stone*, January 24, 2018.

15. "Country Music Rap Sheet—A Picture History of Mugshots and Arrests," SavingCountryMusic.com, July 22, 2013.

16. Carrie B. Fried, "Who's Afraid of Rap? Differential Reactions to Music Lyrics," *Journal of Applied Social Psychology* 29, no. 4 (1999): 705–21.

17. Fried, "Who's Afraid of Rap?," 715–16.

18. Fried, "Who's Afraid of Rap?," 716.

19. Carrie B. Fried, "Bad Rap for Rap: Bias in Reactions to Music Lyrics," *Journal of Applied Social Psychology* 26, no. 23 (1996): 2135–46.

20. Shamena Anwar, Patrick Bayer, and Randi Hjalmarsson, "The Role of Age in Jury Selection and Trial Outcomes," *Journal of Law and Economics* 57, no. 4 (2014): 1001–30.

21. Adam Dunbar et al., "The Threatening Nature of 'Rap' Music," *Psychology, Public Policy, and Law* 22, no. 3 (2016): 288 (emphasis added).

22. For more on the way that listeners perceive sexually explicit content in rap as more offensive than similarly explicit content in other genres, see Travis Dixon and Daniel Linz, "Obscenity Law and Sexually Explicit Rap Music: Understanding the Effects of Sex, Attitudes, and

Beliefs," *Journal of Applied Communication Research* 25, no. 3 (1997): 217–41.

23. Amy Binder, "Constructing Racial Rhetoric: Media Depictions of Harm in Heavy Metal and Rap Music," *American Sociological Review* 58, no. 6 (December 1993): 753–67.

24. Binder, "Constructing Racial Rhetoric," 765.

25. Carrie B. Fried, "Stereotypes of Music Fans: Are Rap and Heavy Metal Fans a Danger to Themselves or Others?," *Journal of Media Psychology* 8, no. 3 (2003): 2–27.

26. Fried, "Stereotypes of Music Fans," abstract.

27. Adam Dunbar and Charis E. Kubrin, "Imagining Violent Criminals: An Experimental Investigation of Music Stereotypes and Character Judgments," *Journal of Experimental Criminology* 14, no. 4 (October 2018): 507–28.

28. John H. Blume, Sheri L. Johnson, and Emily C. Paavola, "Every Juror Wants a Story: Narrative Relevance, Third Party Guilt and the Right to Present a Defense," *American Criminal Law Review* 44 (2007): 1069.

29. *Old Chief v. United States*, 519 U.S. 172 (1997).

30. Blume et al., "Every Juror Wants a Story," 1069.

31. *Darden v. Wainwright*, 477 U.S. 168 (1986).

32. Sheri Lynn Johnson, John H. Blume, and Patrick M. Wilson, "Racial Epithets in the Criminal Process," *Michigan State Law Review* 2011, no. 3 (2011): 755; Sheri Lynn Johnson, "Racial Imagery in Criminal Cases," *Tulane Law Review* 67 (1993): 1739.

33. Melissa Block, "The Racially Charged Meaning Behind the Word Thug," *All Things Considered*, NPR, April 30, 2015.

34. Appellant's Brief, *Brooks v. Mississippi*, 2003 WL 23700266 (p. 46).

4. What About the First Amendment?

1. Bob Bauder, "Pittsburgh Set to Settle Leon Ford Civil Rights Lawsuit for $5.5 million," *Tribune-Review*, January 17, 2018.

2. *United States v. Alvarez*, 567 U.S. 709 (2012).

3. *Federal Communications Commission v. Pacifica Foundation*, 438 U.S. 726 (1978).

4. The Slants, "Our Story," www.theslants.com/biography.

5. *Matal v. Tam*, 582 U.S. ____ (2017).

6. Lily Hirsch, "His Music Was Protest, Not Threat—So Why Is Jamal Knox Still in Jail?," The Establishment, October 13, 2016.

7. *Commonwealth v. Knox*, 190 A.3d 1146 (Pa. 2018).

8. Hirsch, "His Music Was Protest, Not Threat."

9. Alex Zimmerman, "99 Problems: Run-in with Jordan Miles Wasn't First Controversial Incident for Three 99-Car Cops," *Pittsburgh City Paper*, December 17, 2014.

10. Eliott C. McLaughlin, "East Pittsburgh Officer Charged with Criminal Homicide in Antwon Rose Shooting," CNN, June 27, 2018.

11. *Commonwealth v. Knox*, 190 A.3d 1146 (Pa. 2018).

12. Oral Argument, *Elonis v. U.S.*, 575 U.S. ____, December 1, 2014, https://www.supremecourt.gov/oral_arguments/argument_transcripts /2014/13-983_hejm.pdf.

13. Dan Whitcomb, "Sarah Palin Effigy Hung in Halloween Display," Reuters, October 27, 2008; Kimberly Mehlman-Orozco, "Conservatives Forget History with Trump Effigy Outrage," *The Hill*, June 1, 2017.

14. For more on the true threats doctrine as seen through the lens of rap music, see Clay Calvert, Emma Morehart, and Sarah Papadelias, "The True Threats Quagmire: When Does One Man's Lyrics Become Another's Crime?," *Columbia Journal of Law and the Arts* 38 (2014): 1. See also Clay Calvert and Matthew Bunker, "Fissures, Fractures and Doctrinal Drifts: Paying the Price in First Amendment Jurisprudence for a Half Decade of Avoidance, Minimalism and Partisanship," *William and Mary Bill of Rights Journal* 24, no. 4 (2016): 943; Lily Hirsch, "Rap as Threat? The Violent Translation of Music in American Law," *Law, Culture and the Humanities* 14, no. 3 (2018): 482–500.

15. See *Dawson v. Delaware*, 503 U.S. 159 (1992); Dan T. Coenen, "Free Speech and the Law of Evidence," *Duke Law Journal* 68 (2019): 639.

16. Jim Suhr, "Ill. SupCo Takes Pass, Ends Student Threat Case," Associated Press, May 30, 2013.

17. See Coenen, "Free Speech and the Law of Evidence."

18. It was on display during the Supreme Court oral argument in *Elonis v. U.S.* Justice Scalia questioned attorneys for both parties as to whether the lyrics were "valuable" or "not worth a whole lot." Oral Argument, *Elonis v. United States*, December 1, 2014.

19. Carlos F. Ortega, "Narcocorridos," in *Celebrating Latino Folklore: An Encyclopedia of Cultural Traditions*, ed. Mari Herrera-Sobek (Santa Barbara, CA: ABC-CLIO, 2012), 2:831–38.

20. *State v. Hanson*, 46 Wash.App. 656 (1987).

21. See *Hanson v. City of Snohomish*, 121 Wash. 2d 552, 555, 852 P.2d 295, 296 (1993).

22. E.g., *Brown v. State*, No. 1302 Sept. Term 2013, 2016 WL 5720590 (Md. Ct. Spec. App. Sept. 30, 2016); *United States v. Foster*, 939 F.2d 445 (7th Cir. 1991).

23. *United States v. Stuckey*, 253 F. App'x 468, 483 (6th Cir. 2007).

24. *State v. Skinner*, 218 N.J. 496, 500, 95 A.3d 236, 238 (2014); *Hannah v. State*, 420 Md. 339, 23 A.3d 192 (2011).

25. The title of this section is derived from Ice-T's album *The Iceberg/Freedom of Speech . . . Just Watch What You Say!* (Sire, 1989).

26. *Miller v. California*, 413 U.S. 15 (1973).

27. *Skyywalker Records, Inc. v. Navarro*, 739 F. Supp. 578, 591 (S.D. Fla. 1990), *rev'd sub nom. Luke Records, Inc. v. Navarro*, 960 F.2d 134 (11th Cir. 1992).

28. Sara Rimer, "Obscenity or Art? Trial on Rap Lyrics Opens," *New York Times*, October 17, 1990.

29. Chuck Philips, "Appeals Court Voids Obscenity Ruling on 2 Live Crew Album," *Los Angeles Times*, May 8, 1992.

30. *Commonwealth v. Knox*, 190 A.3d 1146, 1151 (Penn. 2018).

5. Aggressive Prosecutors and Untrained Experts

1. Gary Klein, "Sausalito Traffic Stop Leads to Arrest of Antioch Gang Shooting Suspect," *Marin Independent Journal*, November 12, 2012 (updated July 18, 2018).

2. Paul Detrick, "Man Imprisoned for Rap Videos," *Reason*, November 15, 2014.

3. Sam Lefebvre, "Rap's Poetic License: Revoked," *East Bay Express*, April 29, 2015.

4. Lefebvre, "Rap's Poetic License: Revoked."

5. California Penal Code Sec. 215(b) (1993).

6. California Penal Code Sec. 186.22(b)(4)(B).

7. See "Gang-Related Legislation by Subject, Juveniles," National Gang Center, U.S. Department of Justice, https://www.nationalgangcenter.gov/Legislation/Juveniles (last accessed November 8, 2018).

8. See "Brief Review of Federal and State Definitions of the Terms 'Gang,' 'Gang Crime,' and 'Gang Member,'" National Gang Center, U.S. Department of Justice, December 2016.

9. *The CalGang Criminal Intelligence System*, Report 2015-130 (Sacramento, CA: California State Auditor, 2016), 3.

10. Alan Jackson, *Prosecuting Gang Cases: What Local Prosecutors Need to Know* (Arlington, VA: American Prosecutors Research Institute, 2004), 16 (emphasis in original). Jackson was a Los Angeles assistant district attorney when he wrote the manual.

11. Stephanie Francis Ward, "Prosecutors Are Using Rap Music to Convince Jurors of Gang Ties," *ABA Journal*, December 2014.

12. Lefebvre, "Rap's Poetic License: Revoked."

13. Ward, "Prosecutors Are Using Rap Music."

14. Richard Valdemar, "Testifying in Court as a Gang Expert," *Police Magazine*, April 11, 2008.

15. Robert J. Shaughnessy, "Dirty Little Secrets of Expert Testimony," *Litigation* 33, no. 2 (Winter 2007): 47.

16. Charles M. Katz and Vincent J. Webb, Arizona State University West, "Police Response to Gangs: A Multi-Site Study," report prepared for the National Institute of Justice, December 2003, x.

17. Gang Enforcement Company, "Explore Our Courses," https://www.gangenforcement.com/gang-training.html (last accessed May 21, 2019).

18. Placido G. Gomez, "It Is Not So Simply Because an Expert Says It Is So: The Reliability of Gang Expert Testimony Regarding Membership

in Criminal Street Gangs: Pushing the Limits of Texas Rule of Evidence 702," *St. Mary's Law Journal* 34 (2003): 581–622. More broadly, other legal scholars have criticized unscientific police expert testimony on a range of subjects. See, e.g., Anna Lvovsky, "The Judicial Presumption of Police Expertise," *Harvard Law Review* 130, no. 8 (2017): 1995–2081; Brian R. Gallini, "To Serve and Protect? Officers as Expert Witnesses in Federal Drug Prosecutions," *George Mason Law Review* 19, no. 2 (2012): 363–413; Anne Bowen Poulin, "Experience-Based Opinion Testimony: Strengthening the Lay Opinion Rule," *Pepperdine Law Review* 39, no. 3 (2012): 551–618; Maxine D. Goodman, "A Hedgehog on the Witness Stand—What's the Big Idea? The Challenges of Using *Daubert* to Assess Social Science and Nonscientific Testimony," *American University Law Review* 59, no. 3 (2010): 635–684; Joelle Moreno, "What Happens When Dirty Harry Becomes an (Expert) Witness for the Prosecution?," *Tulane Law Review* 79, no. 1 (2004): 1–54.

19. Tim Prudente, "East Baltimore Gang Boss Sentenced to Life in Prison for Ordering the Murder of Police Informant," *Baltimore Sun*, April 30, 2018.

20. Charlie Row Campo, "The Danger Zone," https://www.youtube.com/watch?v=Ij6TJ3chVCg (last accessed November 9, 2018).

21. Fed. R. Evid. 702; *Kumho Tire Co. v. Carmichael*, 526 U.S. 137 (1999); *General Electric v. Joiner*, 525 U.S. 136 (1997); *Daubert v. Merrell Dow Pharmaceuticals*, 509 U.S. 579 (1993).

22. For a discussion of the study, see Joelle Anne Moreno, "Einstein on the Bench? Exposing What Judges Do Not Know About Science and Using Child Abuse Cases to Improve How Courts Evaluate Scientific Evidence," *Ohio State Law Journal* 64 (2003): 531–84.

23. *Commonwealth v. Lamory Gray*, 978 N.E.2d 543 (Mass. 2012).

6. Surveillance, Suppression, and the Rise of Gang Units

1. Twain Gotti, "Ride Out" feat. Mr. Baker, Official Video, YouTube (May 21, 2019).

2. Alyssa Rosenberg, "How Cops and Prosecutors Are Putting Rap on Trial," *Washington Post*, May 21, 2014.

3. William Brangham, "Rap lyrics used as evidence in criminal cases," PBS NewsHour (June 29, 2014).

4. Lynn Langton, "Gang Units in Large Local Law Enforcement Agencies, 2007," NCJ 230071, U.S. Department of Justice, Office of Justice Programs, Bureau of Justice Statistics, October 2010.

5. For a good overview of this research, see Justice Policy Institute, "Gang Wars: The Failure of Enforcement Tactics and the Need for Effective Public Safety Strategies," July 2007, 69–70. It's worth noting, however, that some scholars have found evidence in support of the "realist" view that "surges or trends in the gang problem were actual patterns based on real events rather than media or law enforcement fabrications." See, for example, Gary F. Jensen and Jarrett Thibodeaux, "The Gang Problem: Fabricated Panics or Real Temporal Patterns?," *Homicide Studies* 17, no. 3 (2013): 275–90.

6. Justice Policy Institute, "Gang Wars," 69. See also Charles M. Katz and Vincent J. Webb, Arizona State University West, "Police Response to Gangs: A Multi-Site Study," report prepared for the National Institute of Justice, December 2003, xii, 468.

7. Katz and Webb, "Police Response to Gangs," xii, 468.

8. Andrea Ross, "Killer Poetry in Court," *Frankfurter Allgemeine*, May 21, 2014.

9. K. Babe Howell, "Gang Policing: The Post Stop-and-Frisk Justification for Profile-Based Policing," *University of Denver Criminal Law Review* 5 (2015): 1.

10. Andrew Perrin, "Social Media Usage: 2005–2015," Pew Research Center, October 8, 2015 .

11. Pew Research Center, "Social Media Fact Sheet," February 5, 2018.

12. Ross, "Killer Poetry in Court."

13. Jessica Hopper, "Chicago's Insurgent Rap Scene Is All the Rage, and Chief Keef Is at the Head of It," *Chicago Tribune*, July 27, 2012; Karen McVeigh, "Chicago Hip-Hop Feud Deepens After Death of Joseph 'Lil Jojo' Coleman," *Chicago Tribune*, September 13, 2012.

14. Geoff Harkness, *Chicago Hustle and Flow: Gangs, Gangsta Rap, and Social Class* (Minneapolis: University of Minnesota Press, 2014), 136.

15. Harkness, *Chicago Hustle and Flow*, 137.

16. Geoffrey King, "Meet Tiny Doo, the Rapper Facing Life in Prison for Making an Album," *Guardian*, December 3, 2014.

17. California Penal Code Sec. 182.5 (2000).

18. "A Man Faces Life in Prison for . . . Rapping," American Civil Liberties Union San Diego and Imperial Counties, March 16, 2015.

19. R. Stickney, Steven Luke, and Andie Adams, "Judge Dismisses Gang Conspiracy Charges Against Rapper Tiny Doo," NBC San Diego, March 16, 2015.

20. "A Man Faces Life in Prison for . . . Rapping."

21. Greg Moran, "Dumanis to Resign July 7, Mulls Run for County Board," *San Diego Tribune*, April 21, 2017.

22. Dana Littlefield, "What DA Dumanis Learned After Gang-Conspiracy Cases Sparked Backlash," *San Diego Tribune*, July 9, 2017. In 2018, she expressed similar sentiments in a podcast interview. "The Bonnie Dumanis Interview," *The Voice of San Diego*, May 10, 2018, http://podcast.voiceofsandiego.org/special-podcast-the-bonnie-dumanis-interview.

23. Mark C. Zebrowski and John R. Lanham, "Morrison & Foerster Files Federal Lawsuit on Behalf of Two Men," press release, Morrison & Foerster, LLP, San Diego, January 11, 2017.

24. Bianca Bruno, "Men Lobby Judge to Advance Suit over Botched Gang Arrests," Courthouse News Service, May 22, 2018.

Conclusion

1. Andrea Dennis, "Poetic (In)Justice? Rap Music Lyrics as Art, Life, and Criminal Evidence," 31 *Columbia Journal of Law and the Arts* 1 (2007): 1–41.

2. Dennis, "Poetic (In)Justice?"

3. Fed. R. Evid. 702; *Daubert v. Merrell Dow Pharmaceuticals*, 509 U.S. 579 (1993); *Kumho Tire Co. v. Carmichael*, 526 U.S. 137 (1999); *General Electric v. Joiner*, 525 U.S. 136 (1997).

4. See Joelle Moreno, "What Happens When Dirty Harry Becomes an (Expert) Witness for the Prosecution?," *Tulane Law Review* 79, no. 1

(2004): 1–54. See also Anna Lvovsky, "The Judicial Presumption of Police Expertise," *Harvard Law Review* 130, no. 8 (2017): 1995–2081; Brian R. Gallini, "To Serve and Protect? Officers as Expert Witnesses in Federal Drug Prosecutions," *George Mason Law Review* 19, no. 2 (2012): 363–413. See also the related issue of allowing nonscientific or experience-based expert testimony: Anne Bowen Poulin, "Experience-Based Opinion Testimony: Strengthening the Lay Opinion Rule," *Pepperdine Law Review* 39, no. 3 (2012): 551–618; Maxine D. Goodman, "A Hedgehog on the Witness Stand—What's the Big Idea? The Challenges of Using *Daubert* to Assess Social Science and Nonscientific Testimony," *American University Law Review* 59, no. 3 (2010): 635–84.

5. Fed. R. Evid. 706.

6. *United States v. Gaudin*, 515 U.S. 506 (1995).

7. E.g., Pattern Crim. Jury Instr. 5th Cir. 1.01 (2015); Model Crim. Jury Instr. 8th Cir. 3.04 (2014).

8. You cannot, for example, conduct your own research of facts while sitting on the jury and use that research to decide the case. The judge will instruct as much. But if you already have personal knowledge that affects how you view the facts or evidence admitted, you can use that to make your decision.

9. Paul Butler, *Let's Get Free* (New York: The New Press, 2009).

10. Fair and Just Prosecution (supports newly elected, local, progressive prosecutors), https://fairandjustprosecution.org; Real Justice (a PAC dedicated to electing progressive county prosecutors), https://realjusticepac.org.

11. Adeshina Emmanuel, "Electing Progressive Prosecutors Isn't Enough. Now, Activists Are Holding Them Accountable," *In These Times*, March 26, 2018; Josie Duffie Rice, "Cyrus Vance and the Myth of the Progressive Prosecutor," *New York Times*, October 16, 2017.

12. David Alan Sklansky, "The Progressive Prosecutor's Handbook," *UC Davis Law Review Online* 50 (2017): 25–42; Cleve Wootsen, "Voters Oust Prosecutor Accused of Favoring Ferguson Officer Who Killed Michael Brown," *Washington Post*, August 8, 2018; Ben Austen, "In Philadelphia, a Progressive D.A. Tests the Power—and Learns the

Limits—of His Office," *New York Times Magazine*, October 30, 2018; Alan Greenblatt, "Law and the New Order: A Fresh Wave of District Attorneys Is Redefining Justice," *Governing*, April 2017; Justin Miller, "The New Reformer DAs," *American Prospect*, January 2, 2018.

13. Jessica Pishko, "Can the California Elections Usher in a Slate of Progressive District Attorneys?," *The Nation*, June 5, 2018.

Epilogue

1. Not his real name.

2. Not his real name.

3. Adam Liptak, "Hip-Hop Artists Give the Supreme Court a Primer on Rap Music," *New York Times*, March 6, 2019.

INDEX

ABOUT THE AUTHORS

Erik Nielson is an associate professor of liberal arts at the University of Richmond, where he teaches courses on African American literature and hip hop culture. He lives in Richmond, Virginia, and Brooklyn, New York.

Andrea L. Dennis holds the John Byrd Martin Chair of Law at the University of Georgia School of Law and was formerly an assistant federal public defender. She lives in Athens, Georgia.

PUBLISHING IN THE PUBLIC INTEREST